Diaspora as translation and decolonisation

Manchester University Press

THEORY FOR A GLOBAL AGE

Series Editor: Gurminder K. Bhambra, Professor of Postcolonial and Decolonial Studies in the School of Global Studies, University of Sussex

Globalisation is widely viewed as a current condition of the world, but there is little engagement with how this changes the way we understand it. The Theory for a Global Age series addresses the impact of globalisation on the social sciences and humanities. Each title focuses on a particular theoretical issue or topic of empirical controversy and debate, addressing theory in a more global and interconnected manner. With contributions from scholars across the globe, the series explores different perspectives to examine globalisation from a global viewpoint. True to its global character, the Theory for a Global Age series is available for online access worldwide via Creative Commons licensing, aiming to stimulate wide debate within academia and beyond.

Previously published by Bloomsbury:

Connected sociologies
Gurminder K. Bhambra

Eurafrica: The untold history of European integration and colonialism
Peo Hansen and Stefan Jonsson

On sovereignty and other political delusions
Joan Cocks

Postcolonial piracy: Media distribution and cultural production in the global south
Edited by Lars Eckstein and Anja Schwarz

The Black Pacific: Anti-colonial struggles and oceanic connections
Robbie Shilliam

Democracy and revolutionary politics
Neera Chandhoke

Published by Manchester University Press:

Race and the Yugoslav region: Postsocialist, post-conflict, postcolonial?
Catherine Baker

Debt as power
Tim Di Muzio and Richard H. Robbins

Subjects of modernity: Time-space, disciplines, margins
Saurabh Dube

Frontiers of the Caribbean
Phillip Nanton

John Dewey: The global public and its problems
John Narayan

Bordering intimacy: Postcolonial governance and the policing of family
Joe Turner

Diaspora as translation and decolonisation

Ipek Demir

MANCHESTER UNIVERSITY PRESS

Published by Manchester University Press
Oxford Road, Manchester M13 9PL
www.manchesteruniversitypress.co.uk

British Library Cataloguing-in-Publication Data is available

ISBN 978 1 5261 3468 4 hardback
ISBN 978 1 5261 7873 2 paperback

First published by Manchester University Press in hardback 2022
This edition published 2024

The publisher has no responsibility for the persistence or accuracy of URLs for any external or third-party internet websites referred to in this book, and does not guarantee that any content on such websites is, or will remain, accurate or appropriate.

Typeset by Newgen Publishing UK

Contents

Series editor's foreword

The *Theory for a Global Age* series, of which this important new book is a part, is a space to rethink concepts and categories central to everyday understandings. This is done by taking seriously the experiences and knowledge of those who are rarely seen as agents in such processes. It is also done by re-examining dominant understandings through frameworks and contexts not previously considered. *Diaspora as translation and decolonisation* by Ipek Demir provides a brilliant new account of diaspora in just these terms. She examines the contributions made by the Kurdish diaspora, for example, as well as shifting our focus from the usual concerns of those who study diasporas – 'static' topics such as homeland, identity and questions of belonging – to examine how diasporic communities themselves 'translate, intervene and decolonise' the contexts within and across which they move.

Diasporas are often conceptualised through the politics of nation-states. They are seen to come into being as a consequence of struggles within nations and are represented as coming to reside in what are regarded as the nations of others. In this way, they are presented as having a sense of 'home' elsewhere than where they are. Demir sharply contests such associations. In contrast, she locates diasporas also in the historical relationships consequent to the expansion and dismantling of imperial formations. Drawing on, and extending, Sivanandan's resonant formulation that 'we are here because you were there', she examines both the 'we' and the 'they' in terms of each being diasporic. In the process, she expands our understanding of the term and its associated processes.

Diaspora as translation and decolonisation offers a distinctive and innovative account of the dynamics of diaspora, of the ways in which, for example, they have been involved in processes of decolonisation, albeit rarely recognised as such. Alongside this move, she also points to diaspora as central to modes of translation and intercultural dialogue. She demonstrates the ways in which diasporas unsettle standard conceptions of home and identity, among other understandings, through their social and political interventions across a range of locations. In the process, Demir superbly highlights the difference that new understandings of diaspora can make to the way we think about the global and its ongoing re-figurations.

Gurminder K. Bhambra
University of Sussex

Preface and acknowledgements

A couple of years ago, when I started writing this book, the word 'decolonisation' had not yet become mainstream. It was largely ignored by wider academia and in public debates, despite the fields of decolonial studies and postcolonial studies having made serious interventions questioning Eurocentric assumptions of academia for decades, and despite important social movements such as Black Lives Matter and Decolonise the University having taken off in mid-2010. As an academic who took these interventions seriously, for me the centrality of decolonisation, and the links between diaspora, translation and decolonisation, were clear from the start. I wanted to write a book that captured the transformative and far-reaching role of diaspora, one that sought to expand diasporic imaginary spatially and temporally and show how much could be gained if we weaved translation and decolonisation into understandings of diaspora. The writing of the final sections of the book coincided with the violent killing of George Floyd in 2020 and the rekindling of the Black Lives Matter movement, which during the summer of 2020 turned into a transnational and global phenomenon. We now observe that decolonisation is widely used in popular and academic discourse, both by critics and proponents. The insights of the fields of decolonial studies and postcolonial studies, of race and ethnicity, are receiving increasing and well-deserved attention by wider academia. Many institutions have also begun to reckon with race, including universities of the Global North as they move to decolonise teaching and research. However, the pushback is evident, as shown by the stepping up of culture wars in 2020 and the recent publication of the much-discredited report of the Commission on Race and Ethnic Disparities. The backlash to diaspora, to its decolonisation efforts, is certainly not over.

I am thankful to all those who have contributed intellectually to this book through our conversations, their writings, thoughtful exchanges, feedback and considerations. I would especially like to express my thanks to Professor Gurminder K. Bhambra, my series editor, for her excellent feedback, intellectual rigour and extremely generous support, to Professor John Holmwood, who has been providing intellectual stimulation and depth since he became my PhD supervisor at the University of Sussex, to Professor Martin Kusch, for many conversations about language, translation and incommensurability during my postdoctoral fellowship at the University of Cambridge, to Professor Barbara Misztal at the University of Leicester, whose intellectual breadth and depth always inspired me, to Professor John Holmwood, Professor Barbara Misztal, Dr Pierre Monforte and Dr Ebru Soytemel for their constructive comments on various chapters, and of course to all my colleagues at the University of Leeds and the Centre for Ethnicity and Racism Studies (CERS) for stimulating discussions and productive exchanges over the last two years. I am very grateful to Professor Robin Cohen for his thoughtful and insightful feedback, suggestions and encouragement. I would like to thank my publishers, Manchester University Press, especially Thomas Dark and Alun Richards for their ongoing support and professionalism, and also for their patience when I was unwell. I would also like to thank Susan Jarvis for her very helpful and meticulous editing.

I am grateful to my family in Turkey who instilled in me a strong sense of justice, which underpins all my work, and to Andy for his unending support and generosity. The work for this book was supported by the Arts and Humanities Research Council (AHRC) Fellowship Programme and subsequent research. I would like to thank my research participants for their generosity and support.

The book is for those who care about diaspora and who seek recognition of how diasporas have conceptually and practically expanded ideas about equality and freedom and dignity. It is a book for those who wish to not only develop a decolonial perspective to diaspora, but also seek to recognise how diasporas are primary agents of decolonisation of the Global North.

Introduction

This book draws our attention to the concept of diaspora and investigates it both theoretically and empirically. It analyses how diasporas can translate, decolonise and pierce exclusive nationalisms. As such, it provides a discussion of what a theory of diaspora for our global age should prioritise, revealing its transformative and far-reaching potential. My thinking through of diaspora is unashamedly concerned with diaspora as an analyst category rather than being an examination of how actors deploy it strategically and discursively to gain political advantage. If diaspora is to have an analytical purchase, it should be employed when illuminating a particular and specific angle of migration or migrancy. It should valorise and inquire into a particular aspect of migration. The aspect I defend in this book is how diasporas do translation and decolonisation.

Since the first decade of the twenty-first century, we have seen nativist movements and anti-immigration sentiments becoming more mainstream and alarmingly moving to centre-stage. There has been a major shift, especially in the Global North, including from certain sections of the left (Bloomfield, 2020; Mondon and Winter, 2019; Shilliam, 2020). Nativists are reacting not only to economic globalisation, but also to racial, cultural and religious diversity, equality and multiculturalism at home. The reactions are related: they are both to do with feelings of loss of sovereignty and control. These two types of loss of sovereignty and control – one globally and one at home – are also brought together through 'diaspora'. Diaspora is deeply interlinked with sovereignty, belonging and transnationalism, and also ideologies and sentiments of 'imperialistic abroad and xenophobic at home' (Venuti, 1995: 23).

Many nativist movements and anti-immigration sentiments, current and past, show a longing for the good old times when the Global North set the rules of the international order, held the upper hand in world trade and was able to migrate and settle in others' lands, often through the use of brutal force. Longing is clear and visible in the slogans of many of the movements in the Global North: 'Make the Netherlands Great Again' (Wilder's slogan); 'Austria First' (the campaign message of Hofer's Freedom Party); 'Putting the "Great" Back into Great Britain' (the UKIP Manifesto slogan); 'Make America Great Again' (Trump's 2020 slogan); and 'Take Back Control' (the Leave campaign during Brexit). A sense of insecurity and anxiety about declining privileges and a feeling of victimhood, paradoxically combined with a sense of superiority and exceptionalism (Melville, 2020) underwrite the recent nativist movements, but also those that preceded them. However, it would be a mistake to narrowly conceive such current, past and also future nativisms and movements in the Global North as being limited to the crisis on new migrations – notwithstanding their importance. Such sentiments are in fact often closely linked to resentments towards settled diasporas of colour in the Global North. Anxieties about loss of control and sovereignty are deeply intertwined with existing diasporas of colour in the Global North and the decolonisations and translations they bring – the central themes of this book.

Empires have governed various populations, myriad ethnic, religious and cultural groups. Through plantations, indenture, colonisation, expansion, settlements, slavery and other forms of domination and movements of peoples, empires have been instigators of diasporas. Many of today's diasporas were made in and by recent empires, including the collapse of them and/or the nationalist projects that followed them – the Ottoman Empire (e.g. Kurdish and Armenian diasporas); the Austro-Hungarian Empire (e.g. Slavic and Jewish diasporas); the British Empire (e.g. Afro-Caribbean and South-Asian diasporas); and the French Empire (e.g. Arab diaspora). Many of today's diasporas are thus an outcome of historic relationships arising out of subordination and colonisation, of expansion and retraction of empires. Much recent diaspora literature and the ever-expanding case studies of diaspora, however, examine diaspora within the confines of nation-states. Diaspora is understood as emerging out of 'ethno-political' struggles within nation-states, and often told from a perspective of push factors. This has happened despite many diaspora theorists, for example, Avtar Brah, Robin Cohen, Paul Gilroy, Stuart Hall and others having discussed diaspora within the context of empire. This has had consequences for diaspora research, as it has brought limitations to understandings of diaspora. The links between empire and diaspora are too often ignored, and the transnational dimensions of diaspora research are curtailed. As such, the temporal and spatial boundaries and imaginations of diaspora research are capped.

Diaspora research has often ended up being too tightly hemmed into the history, sources and understandings of the nation-state. Yet today's diasporas are products of empires as much as of nation-states. Much of the literature on the case studies of diaspora and diaspora theorising at times ends up producing methodologically nationalist discourses and examinations. They often focus on case studies, as identified by Faist (2010: 25), without necessarily informing how the case study can expand or challenge the way we have conceptualised diaspora. Ironically, this occurs despite the close affinity diaspora has with the literature on transnationalism. As the links between empire and diaspora are ignored, the consequences of expansions and retractions are erased. Nation-state centric approaches to diaspora multiply. Diaspora should instead be understood as inscribed and entangled in a series of historical and political processes associated with empire and expansion – including, of course, nationalist and ethno-political responses to these. Ethno-political struggles and diasporisation – that is, their spilling over into other places – are a postcolonial phenomenon. Even if we take an example like the Kurds, which typically is constructed within nation-centric discourses, it is not possible to understand Kurds and the Kurdish diaspora without an awareness of the role of the Ottoman, French and British empires, and their reorganisation of the borders and consolidation of populations and religious and ethnic allegiances in the Middle East. Nor can a perspective that ignores empire place Kurdish diaspora and its activities within a Global South perspective, or identify and unpack Kurdish indigenous and decolonial discourses arising in diaspora – approaches I have been able to utilise. Instead region-centric, nation-state and security-dominated perspectives continue to dominate the field. Such a turn to empire is also needed to uncover the imperialist origins of the field of Kurdish studies, which were forged by imperialist projects – amongst others, the 'Russian, British and French consuls and intelligence officers' (Bruinessen, 2013: 1).

Confining discussions of diaspora to the politics of 'their' nation-state also places boundaries on diaspora's citizenship in the new home, leaving a question mark over the extent to which they can belong. It continues to reproduce the assumption that the real home of diasporas remains elsewhere – that is, their nation-state – with the consequence that their citizenship in the new home is regarded as contingent and revokable, even when there are centuries of linkages and lineages that were created through empire, as expressed in the well-known phrase 'we are here because you were there'. We can think of how those from the Windrush generation in Britain were regarded as 'immigrants' despite the fact that they were coming to the 'mother country'. Or that the French army in World War II was two-thirds or more African, yet not only was their significant role in the liberation of France and the defeat of Nazism denied, but they were also refused French army pensions.[1] Leaving the relationship between empire and diaspora unacknowledged and unexplored can mean that even those diasporas that have extremely close historical and cultural links with the metropole can continue to be construed as an 'other' and their presence questioned. They can even be turned from 'citizens into migrants' through citizenship legislation (Karatani, 2003), as we saw in the case of Windrush.

Additionally, an understanding that breaks the link between empire and diaspora overlooks how diasporas can become agents of decolonisation. For it is not only that diasporas have their roots in recent empires: they increasingly throw up multicultural problems for the metropole as they seek to undo unequal and hierarchical relationships entrenched in empire, a central focus of this book. Diaspora is therefore the nemesis of collective amnesia, questioning the spatial and temporal limitations imposed on it. Asymmetric colonial systems come to be challenged and reconfigured through the decolonisations carried out by diasporas. Through a conceptualisation of diaspora as translation and decolonisation, this book resists the confinement and reduction of diaspora theorisation to the nation-state. It spatially and temporally seeks to expand diasporic imaginary and shows much can be gained if we weave translation and decolonisation into understandings of diaspora.

The literature on diasporas spans various disciplines and fields. Diaspora is a concept that has been housed, examined and applied in many disciplines – politics, international relations, literature, sociology, geography, language, history, media and others. Moreover, some diaspora research is interdisciplinary. It is therefore a challenging task to group and engage with it with precision. It is well known that the concept itself has 'diasporised' (Brubaker, 2005). In this book, I develop a critical engagement with two dominant forms of diaspora theorising. One is what I call the 'ideal type' approach led by Cohen, Safran and others devoted to identifying the key characteristics of diaspora (e.g. Cohen, 1996; Safran, 1991). The second is what I call the 'hybridity' approach (e.g. Bhabha, 1994; Brah, 1996; Clifford, 1994; Gilroy, 1993; Hall, 1990). Both approaches have indeed helped to clarify our understandings of diaspora. The clarity, rigour and insights of Cohen's elaborations have been extremely important, and Hall, Gilroy and Brah have opened up other new and innovative ways of thinking about diaspora. The second group's focus on fluidity, subjectivity and hybridity attempted to undo and readjust the first group's definitional focus, which was accused of being too locked into the gardening tropes of roots, origin and soil. Despite the important links it developed between empire and diaspora, the latter approach to diaspora is not fully satisfactory either: if all cultures are basically hybrid, fluid and shaped by subjectivity, little can be gained from identifying that diasporas are too. Moreover, the focus of these two approaches – one on 'being' and the other on 'becoming' – has at times too narrowly confined diaspora theorising to ontological concerns.

Rather than seeing diaspora as an everlasting feature of a group, or as centred around a subjective fluid experience, I focus on the interventions diasporas make, namely how diasporas do translation and decolonisation in their new home and the home left behind. I thus seek to change the terms of discussion on diaspora. Such a conceptualisation affords heterogeneity and temporality to our applications of diaspora, instead of all members and actions of a group being stamped with 'diaspora', and for eternity. Such a temporal and heterogeneous calibration of the concept of diaspora and its employment questions the essentialism and primordialism often associated with the notion of diaspora. Yet it seeks to refrain from confining it to subjectivity, often associated with the hybridity approach. I aim to develop an understanding of diaspora that reveals its capacity as a critical concept, claiming its transformative and far-reaching potential.

A focus on the dynamics of diaspora as translation and diaspora as decolonisation, I argue, can expand thinking and understanding of diaspora within the current dynamics of our globalised world. Translation is not just a useful metaphor for understanding the movement and struggles of diasporas; more importantly, translation studies has much insight, from which we can learn, apply and extend our understandings in diaspora studies. I discuss 'diaspora as translation' (Chapter 2) together with 'diaspora as decolonisation' (Chapter 3). I propose a new and productive way of conceptualising diaspora, drawing from the insights of translation studies to inform understandings of authenticity, untranslatability and incommensurability. Diasporas are the archetypal translators, as they put new identities, languages and world-views in circulation. They can also erase, domesticate and rewrite. Anthropologists have also paid attention to translation when unpacking hierarchies arising from European expansion and colonisation. My focus on translation turns the tables on this. I pay attention to how, this time, we can examine the flows of peoples and cultures going to the Global North, but more importantly, how they 'speak back' to the metropole and dislodge coloniality. This is because, in my conceptualisation, diasporas emerge as central agents for decolonisation of the Global North, but also of Northern regimes elsewhere too – although the former is the focus of this book. I thus see diaspora as a source of liberation of progress. Yet decolonisation and foreignisation – that is, strategies aimed at pushing the boundaries of the target rather than simply assimilating into it – are difficult. In Chapter 2, therefore, I examine the lure of translation for diaspora, unpacking 'diaspora as rewriting and transformation', 'diaspora as erasure and exclusion' and 'diaspora as a tension between foreignisation and domestication'.

Ricoeur (2006) sees linguistic hospitality as a model for other forms of hospitality. Diasporas translate their identity struggles and battles to the host. Such translations can take place in the form of foreignisation or domestication; they can be partial and at times opaque. They can smooth over differences, leave out sections and at other times help to achieve 'unlearning'. But, as I explore in the book, through foreignisation strategies, diasporas have been, and continue to remain, agents of decolonisation. Such a focus on diasporas and their translation of identity is tied inextricably to their battles in the new homes, transnationally but also back in the home left behind. It can thus help to expand diaspora research, which has tended to focus on methodologically nationalist understandings, examining single-case studies without much situating the case study in wider social, political and global debates of our times, or history or empire, or informing how the case study can expand or challenge how we have conceptualised diaspora so far through offering new heuristic and conceptual tools. Hence it is not that case studies of a particular diasporic group are used often, but *how* they are used that has become the problem. It is time we turn attention to how diasporas have intervened in and shaped the culture and debates globally.

It should be clear by now that in this book I am not focusing on textual translation of diasporas, nor am I examining literary works to do with diasporas. I am taking people, identity and power rather than text as my primary source for uncovering diasporic translations. The aim of the book is to provoke a new thinking of diaspora that is political, and engaged with the contemporary global order by using the insights of translation studies and research on migrancy, race and culture. Diasporas can unsettle and trouble North-centric visions and Northern epistemologies. This is why, in Chapter 3, I argue that we need to shift our focus to an exploration of how diasporas decolonise the Global North.

Diasporas bring various disruptions and destabilisations to the Global North. I see the provincialising and decolonising carried out by postcolonial diasporas as a form of 'talking back' to the metropole, and discuss them in detail in Chapter 3. I start with a discussion of how vertical fallacies were created by Victorian anthropologists in their translations of 'others'. The chapter argues that diasporas should not simply be seen as mediators but as agents who speak back and challenge the world-views in the Global North, aiding foreignisation and decolonisation of the new home. They also speak back and challenge world-views in the home left behind, aiding decolonisation of the homeland at a distance. I conceptualise how diasporas undo colonisation through two central processes – 'radical remembering' and 'radical inclusion' – which I posit against 'social inclusion' through a focus on the United Kingdom example.

I thus make the case that diasporic decolonisations, such as the Bristol Bus Boycott (1963), the Imperial Typewriters Strike (1974), the Grunwick Dispute (1976), the activism following the New Cross Fire (1981), the mobilisations following the Grenfell Fire (2017), the Windrush Scandal (2018), the Black Lives Matter movement and many others, are examples of how diasporas challenge and expand understandings of freedom, equality and dignity in the metropole and globally. Thus, rather than repeat 'the tyranny of in-betweenness', the often-used and tired metaphors and imagery of diaspora as being stuck between the home and the host, as peoples constantly straddling two cultures, falling through gaps, my focus is on how diasporas of colour do translation and decolonisation in the Global North, on how they intervene and shape. Even though many of my examples and most of my focus are based on diasporas in the Global North, especially in the United Kingdom, I provide plenty of conceptual tools and positive heuristic devices for investigating diasporas in general.

Having provided examples of the decolonisation demands of South Asian and Afro-Caribbean diasporas in the United Kingdom for 'radical inclusion' and 'radical remembering' in Chapter 3, I turn to an analysis of the translational activities, interventions and undoings of the Kurdish diaspora in Europe in Chapter 4. Using empirical data from my own research on the Kurdish diaspora in Europe I unpack how those in the Kurdish diaspora carry out ethno-political translations of their struggle and how such translations are central for the transnational battles of Kurds. I examine how they rewrite Kurdish politics, undo colonisation and carry out both foreignisations and domestication in their engagements with the Global North, exposing links between their predicament, Europe and colonialism. The chapter rethinks the Kurdish diaspora globally by examining it as 'transnational indigenous resistance' and thus entangled in a series of historical and political processes associated with empire, expansion, expulsion and appropriation, including nationalist and ethno-political responses to these. I explore how an indigenous identity is being anchored by translations and decolonisations of the Kurdish diaspora – that is, by those who initially had to dis-anchor themselves from their homeland. As such, I uproot indigeneity, yet embed transnationality and diasporicity. By centring my discussion of Kurdish diaspora on empires, indigeneity and transnationalism, I also move discussions of diaspora from nation-centric and state-centric discussions which have dominated the field of Kurdish studies. I thus expand the spatial and temporal dimensions of research on Kurdish diaspora. Although I am careful and refrain from making generalisations to other diasporas, some of the analytical points I develop are relevant and portable (Polit and Beck, 2010) to other settings and diasporas, where there is a close link between colonialism, indigeneity and a strong desire to translate ethno-political identity.

Diaspora considered as translation and decolonisation in this book does not valorise transnationalism or migrancy as transformative. It argues that diaspora is a special case of migration and transnationalism whereby politicised decolonial subjectivity is associated with mobility. Diaspora, then, is not just about migration or the movement of peoples in general. As I discuss, what transforms 'overseas' people who migrate into a diaspora is that they 'speak back' to the metropole or the homeland, and engage in the dislodging of coloniality. Instead of using the term 'diaspora' synonymously with 'ethnicity' or 'race', the conceptualisation I offer recognises that certain migrant groups can become diasporic over time (and vice versa) – for example, Kurds who were 'migrants' became a 'Kurdish diaspora' over time in Europe, or how Poles went from being seen as a 'diaspora' in the 1950s into being regarded as 'migrants' in the 2000s in Europe. We therefore need to recognise that diasporas are not only the products of globalisation and decolonisation (or movements to the 'motherland'); they are also the agents and makers of globalisation and of decolonisation. Their translations and decolonisations, their interventions, often make them unpopular not just in the home left behind but also in the new home. In Europe, they become what I conceive as 'the Global South in the Global North'. This is why, in Chapter 5, I turn to an examination of the backlash to diaspora in the Global North. Anti-immigration sentiments in the Global North are in fact closely bound up with, if not at times used as a proxy for, discomfort and resentment towards settled diasporas of colour in the Global North, and most importantly against their demands for equality. Worries about new migrations are closely entangled with anxieties about existing diasporas of colour in the Global North, tied to alienations and resentments associated with dominant hegemonic nationals' declining privileges and status.

Chapter 5 examines this backlash to diaspora and thinks through the attempts to 'write out' diasporas of colour in the Global North through discourses of anti-multiculturalism and 'the left-behind'/ 'traditional' working class. While anti-multiculturalism discredits the equality demands of some, the discourse of 'the left-behind'/ 'traditional' working class comes to define the working class, and those who need help and support, as White. Such discourses render diasporas of colour as classless while at the same time positing them as having 'too much culture and identity' and as a threat to the nation. Both discourses are expressions of exclusive nationalism as they signal and reproduce the idea that some ethnic groups belong to Britain, France, the Netherlands – or the West in general – more than others. They conflate national identity (e.g. American, French, British) with the hegemonic ethnic and racial group (e.g. European descent in America, White English in Britain). Understandings of the country and national identity thus become indistinguishable from this hegemonic ethnic and racial group. Such discourses not only erase diasporas of colour from the narrative of the working class and accounts of the nation, but also render their demands for equality and inclusion as divisive and a threat. Often applied together, such discourses reject diasporas of colour as legitimate and equal members of the nation while in the same breath accusing them of not integrating and creating 'parallel lives'.

It is perhaps no coincidence that anti-multiculturalism reached its peak at a time when minoritised groups were catching up and when social distance between groups in the United Kingdom was identified as decreasing (e.g. Heath and Demireva, 2014), and that the discourse of 'the left-behind'/'traditional' working class as a codeword for the White working class has emerged as the working class in the Global North is increasingly made up of racialised migrants and people of colour. Chapter 5 thinks through why these discourses have had such a purchase in wider political, media and academic debates, and how they reproduce exclusive nationalisms. It discusses the close relationship between 'getting high' on national identity and the decline in racial and ethnic privilege and status. It traces the salience of discourses of anti-multiculturalism and 'the left-behind'/'traditional' working class, and how they disarm and bypass racialised ways of talking, yet still exhibit a clear concern with hegemonic ethnic and racial identities (Whiteness in the Global North). It examines how they are deployed when resisting loss of sovereignty at home via signalling the forgotten Whites. I argue that, together, they serve to maintain exclusive (White) nationalisms in the Global North.

This book seeks to shift the terms of the discussion of diaspora away from a focus on homeland, hybridity and subjectivity to explore the ways in which diasporas translate, intervene and decolonise. It critically engages with existing theories of diaspora, including perspectives that have tended to lock diaspora to homeland politics and nation-states, as well as perspectives that valorise diasporic subjectivity and hybridity, and trap it into discussions of in-betweenness. The book instead seeks to spatially and temporally expand the boundaries of diaspora thinking by providing examples of how diasporas dislodge coloniality, question hierarchical relationships and coloniality, and reconfigure new transnational formations – for example, indigenous transnationalism. Even though my case study (of Kurds) and examples focus on diasporas in Europe, as the 'Global South in the Global North', the conceptual interventions I make can be applied to other parts of the world, to other places and cases – for example, to the Chinese diaspora in Malaysia, the Irish diaspora in the United States or the Haitian diaspora in Brazil. By introducing concepts such as 'diaspora as rewriting and transformation', 'diaspora as erasure and exclusion', 'diaspora as a tension between foreignisation and domestication', 'radical remembering' and 'radical inclusion', the chapters that follow provide new tools for diaspora research and a framework for understanding diaspora as a specific angle of migration. The book seeks to go beyond a discussion of diaspora based on homeland ties, subjectivity and hybridity, and instead presents an enhanced case for the role of diaspora in the global age through a focus on how, through their translations and decolonisations, diasporas bring disruptions and destablisations to racialised hierarchies and global orders.

Note

1 Non-White French colonial troops were also intentionally excluded from the liberation of Paris (and the famous liberation pictures), referred to as Blanchiment (Whitening).

1

Theories of diaspora and their limitations

i will be african
even if you want me to be german
and i will be german
even if my blackness does not suit you

(May Ayim, 2003)

The 1990s was a time of revival for studies of diaspora – it could be termed the heyday of diaspora theorisation. As well as the books published on diaspora in this period, the journal *Diaspora: A Journal of Transnational Studies* was established in 1991, and debates on diaspora proliferated not just in this journal but in many others. The focus was on transnationalism and dispersion. Khachig Tölölyan, who established this journal, later said, 'If I were establishing the journal now, its subtitle might be "a journal of dispersion studies"' (Tölölyan, 2019: 23). As this book will show, it is appropriate that he named it "diaspora". Study of diaspora should be much more than dispersion. It is also about assemblage and collectiveness, and of intervening and decolonising.

When looking back at the work published during this period, we can see that two main trends emerged with regard to diaspora theorisation in the 1990s. These two approaches have come to dominate diaspora research since then. I term one the 'ideal type approach'. This approach was led by Cohen, Safran and others, who devoted much attention to identifying the key characteristics of diaspora (Cohen, 1996; Safran, 1991). They attempted to answer questions such as: Who and under what conditions does a group become a diaspora? Who should count as diaspora? Is the theme of 'return' central to diasporas? What types of diasporas are there besides 'victim' ones? It was through questions such as these that theorists thought through the key characteristics of diaspora. I refer to the second approach as the 'hybridity' approach. Scholars ranging from Hall to Gilroy to Brah examined diaspora in a dynamic way, ensuring that they steered clear of the gardening tropes of roots, soil and origin. Their works attempted to go beyond what they saw as essentialist understandings of identity and diaspora, instead placing hybridity, ambiguity and fluidity at the centre of our understanding of diaspora. While the first group examined what can be referred to as 'diaspora as a being', this second group focused on 'diaspora as a becoming'. I will take up these two central branches of diaspora theorisation and discuss their central contributions, but also their shortcomings, by critically engaging with them. In the following chapters, I will propose a different way of thinking about diaspora to make the concept of diaspora more relevant for understanding the contemporary global age.

Diaspora theorised as an ideal type: 'Diaspora as a being'

The term 'diaspora' means 'to sow widely; to scatter seeds'. It was used originally to refer to the movement/displacement of Greeks, and their move to Asia Minor, and was closely linked to conquest, migration and gain (Cohen, 1996: 507–8) rather than notions of loss and exile. The Greek use thus centred on the notion of spreading from an original homeland but looking for gain and conquest. In the Judeo-Christian tradition, the concept of diaspora came to be used to refer to the exile of Jews after the Babylonian destruction of the temple in Jerusalem. This became a paradigmatic case of the way this concept was applied. Diaspora has been used most extensively when referring to the dispersal of Jewish peoples from their homeland, and thus became closely linked to loss and displacement. In the twentieth century, it gradually came to be applied to dispersed groups – for example, Irish, Armenians, Palestinians and Africans with experiences such as famine, genocide, slavery, erasure and denial. Its popularity in international relations over the last 25 years has made it a close ally, if not an extension, of the concept of nation, and its popularity in sociology has allied it closely with ethnicity, hybridity and belonging.

Diaspora theorising and empirical research on diaspora flourished in the late 1980s and 1990s. Diaspora theorising proposed key criteria for diasporas. Sheffer's (1986) typology of diaspora revolved around ethnicity, homeland and hostland, diaspora as an entity, and diaspora as a group of peoples. Following on from Sheffer's typology, diaspora came to be conceptualised through the deployment of Weberian ideal types. Safran, and later Cohen, presented key definitions and criteria for diasporas.

Safran identified and summarised the key aspects of diaspora (1991: 83–4):

1. They, or their ancestors, have been dispersed from a specific original 'center' to two or more 'peripheral', or foreign regions.
2. They retain a collective memory, vision or myth about their original homeland – its physical location, history and achievements.
3. They believe that they are not – and perhaps cannot be – fully accepted by their host society, and therefore feel partly alienated and insulated from it.
4. They regard their ancestral homeland as their true, ideal home and as the place to which they or their descendants would (or should) eventually return – when conditions are appropriate.
5. They believe that they should, collectively, be committed to the maintenance or restoration of their original homeland and to its safety and prosperity.
6. They continue to relate, personally or vicariously, to that homeland in one way or another, and their ethno-communal consciousness and solidarity are importantly defined by the existence of such a relationship.

Safran's list represented a landmark by identifying dispersal, the idea of a homeland and the idea of a new home, as well as identity and collective memory, as central. For Safran, diaspora needs to be used for minorities if they display several of these characteristics. As has been pointed out (e.g. Clifford, 1994; Cohen, 1996; Wahlbeck, 2002), however, these characteristics are too restraining in that many groups (e.g. Jews) that are traditionally regarded as a diaspora could in fact be left out if Safran's 'checklist' were followed.

Cohen (1996: 515) later consolidated Safran's list and presented key characteristics of diaspora. This consolidated approach lists features of diasporas as:

1. Dispersal from an original homeland – often traumatically – to two or more foreign regions.
2. Alternatively, the expansion from a homeland in search of work, in pursuit of trade or to further colonial ambitions.
3. A collective memory and myth about the homeland, including its location, history and achievements.
4. An idealisation of the putative ancestral home and a collective commitment to its maintenance, restoration, safety and prosperity – even to its creation.
5. The development of a return movement that gains collective approbation.
6. A strong ethnic group consciousness sustained over a long time and based on a sense of distinctiveness, a common history and the belief in a common fate.
7. A troubled relationship with host societies, suggesting a lack of acceptance at the least, or the possibility that another calamity might befall the group.
8. A sense of empathy and solidarity with co-ethnic members in other countries of settlement.
9. The possibility of a distinctive yet creative and enriching life in host countries with a tolerance for pluralism.

Cohen and Safran's theorising and contributions have been seminal and have cemented the foundations of diaspora research since the 1990s. They clarified understandings and developed an ideal type of diaspora in the Weberian sense. Yet, while they sought to bring ontological clarifications, this has had consequences for subsequent diaspora research. Ideal types are fictional in nature; they are not constructions of common features that arise from empirical research. An ideal type is an abstraction of features, and these features do not need to exist in a pure form. The creation of ideal types is an outcome of not only abstraction, but also of idealisation. An ideal type is not the same as, or even close to, a hypothesis. It does not have much explanatory power or heuristic potential.[1] It instead tasks researchers to fit and measure the world to the ideal type, the abstraction. Holmwood and Stewart (1991: 72) have challenged the heuristic potential of ideal types, and they critically identify that, for Weber, the fact that 'the lack of [ideal types'] application in no way detracts from their conceptual "purity" or value as interpretations'.

Despite their shortcomings, ideal types dominate the field of economics in the social sciences. That markets work (or should work) in a gender-neutral or race-blind way is an ideal type construction, when in fact we know that the market is highly gendered and far from racially neutral. In sociology and politics, Weber has examined bureaucracy and capitalism as ideal types. While ideal types hope to reduce chaos and bring order to the social world, and allow researchers to construct abstractions and meaning, they can create many more problems. The main one is that, in the social sciences – unlike theories in the natural sciences – ideal types are not constructed so they have a general validity. They do not need to be found anywhere in reality before they are applied as an analytical tool. Despite the glaring deviations, and many counter-examples in the social sciences, the ideal type can stay intact.

The use of ideal types and the formulation of diaspora have been welcomed by diaspora scholars (e.g. Wahlbeck, 2002: 230). However, I argue that the centrality of ideal types in diaspora theorising has had several limiting consequences for our understanding of diasporas. First, Safran and Cohen's discussions of the features of diasporas, as with the use of any ideal types, do not have a general validity. They are neither derived from empirical data nor necessarily aimed towards it. As such, diaspora discussed as a Weberian ideal type has features that are either too loosely constructed (e.g. Brubaker's) or too strictly conceptualised (e.g. Safran's), limiting their use for empirical examination of diasporas. Safran and Cohen have rightly and humbly pointed out that no single diaspora will fulfil the features they have identified. It should therefore not surprise us that the 'six traits advanced [by Safran] with such diligence and authority at the start of the project is gradually eroded by the "test" cases he subjects to analysis' (Mishra, 2006: 42). Safran's model also ends up excluding the Jewish diaspora, which he describes as 'the' ideal type (Boyarin and Boyarin, 2003; Clifford, 1997).

Second, ideal types start with abstractions and often put a lid on the reconstructions of these abstractions. As Weber stated, the occasional absence of the concrete individual phenomena is a characteristic of ideal types. In other words, it is not a reason to rethink the ideal type. Ideal types can thus misdirect the research aims, as they task researchers to fit the world to the ideal type features rather than inviting them to reconstruct and reformulate the ideal type abstractions. Cohen (1997), for example, provides a typology of diaspora: victim diaspora, imperial diaspora, cultural diaspora, trade diaspora and labour diaspora. This typology in fact ends up working as a proxy for ethnicity: British constitute an imperial diaspora; Chinese and Lebanese are examples of trading diaspora; Caribbeans represent cultural diaspora; Armenians, Africans and Jews constitute victim diaspora; Indians are labour diaspora. But even though many diasporas can be hyphenated – such as victim-labour (e.g. Kurds) or cultural-trading (e.g. Chinese) – these are not included or accommodated in the theorisation (Mishra, 2006: 46). In diaspora theorising, newer formulations that develop the former typology have not, since Cohen's refinement, taken hold, despite new characteristics being identified (e.g. Shuval, 2000). This has occurred despite diaspora research itself having taken off since then.

Third, ideal types cannot easily account for social change or transformation, and also lack a temporal dimension. In terms of diaspora theorising, ideal type constructions cannot easily accommodate the transformations experienced by diasporic communities. Diasporas and their battles and categories might transform, but diasporic ideal types remain 'as ideal types'. This is why Tsuda (2019) has defended 'diasporicity'. Instead of having debates about ideal characterisation of diasporas, and assessments of whether an ethnic group is diasporic, Tsuda (2019) argues that all dispersed ethnic groups should be accepted as diasporas. He proposes that the diasporicity of these groups is assessed – for example, arguing that victim diasporas have higher levels of diasporicity. However helpful this may be, it brings us back to the original problem of researchers having to assess, measure and fit the world into ideal type features. Ideal types can thus end up being inherently conservative and reify problematic constructions, as Bhambra (2014: 146–50) shows with respect to understandings of modernity. They start with an abstraction and inevitably end up concretising that abstraction, as they are not expected to be tested by empirical data or refuted.

Last but not least, despite its initial clarifications, diaspora studied and constructed as an ideal type has partially limited our ability to think about diaspora globally and to situate the relevance of diaspora in the contemporary world. Diaspora theorising needs to be connected intimately to the movements of peoples that arise from empires expanding and contracting, colonialism, nation-building and slavery, as such dislocations are central to the global political order in which we live today. Yet, so far, diaspora research has focused attention on the diasporic group rather than the context in which diasporas find themselves (e.g. the Global South/North axis) and how they intervene and shape it. We are thus left with a 'slack methodological device' (Cohen, 1996: 515) and, in my view, a conservative form of theorising that has not made transformation or global political ordering central to an understanding of diasporas. The idea that leading diasporic conflicts today are intimately connected to the process of empire, subsequent nation-building, colonialism and decolonisation has tended to be amiss, or at least has not taken centre stage.

Diaspora theorised through hybridity and as subjectivity: 'Diaspora as a becoming'

Another branch of diaspora theorisation had also begun to emerge in the 1990s (e.g. Bhabha, 1994; Brah, 1996; Clifford, 1994; Gilroy, 1993; Hall, 1990). In fact, some of these works preceded the ideal type constructions of diaspora discussed above. Scholars[2] who focused on processes, on becoming and hybridity, instead based their discussions of diaspora in and around notions of transformation, heterogeneity and anti-essentialism, and to some extent on disruption, but especially on diaspora as a mode of cultural production.[3] One main strength of this tradition was its centralisation of the complexities of empire, ethnicity, race and culture rather than, for example, a focus on the importance of the ancestral land or the original homeland for an understanding of diaspora. The other strength was the gendering of the concept of diaspora using an intersectional lens (e.g. Anthias, 1998; Brah, 1996, 2018; Dwyer, 2000; Hussain, 2005; Yuval-Davis, 2011). Some demanded that diaspora be understood more as a condition of subjectivity and less as a type of group, an entity (Anand, 2018; Cho, 2007), while others promoted a flexible use of diaspora as a process that brought the individual and collective together (Mavroudi, 2008). Anthias (2001: 638), on the other hand, presented a strong critique of hybridity, arguing that it marginalised 'materialist, as opposed to culturalist, bases of racist subordinations, inequalities and exclusions' and called for an exploration of intersectional aspects and of trans-ethnic alliances.

'Diaspora as a becoming' focused on processes, and on subjective experiences. Its proponents were thus able to emphasise fluidity and ambiguity, and call for conviviality and creolisation. They questioned ethnic absolutism, and aimed to transcend and transgress essentialised understandings of race, ethnicity and culture. They called for reflexivity with regard to identity, displacement, borders and movement.

Stuart Hall's (1996) influential work, for example, focused on positioning, not essence. He reconstructed a complex and sophisticated understanding of cultural identity, and a non-essentialist understanding of race. For Hall:

> identities are never unified and, in late modern times, increasingly fragmented and fractured; never singular but multiply constructed across different, often intersecting and antagonistic, discourses, practices and positions. They are subject to a radical historicisation, and are constantly in the process of change and transformation.
>
> (Hall, 1996: 17)

He saw cultural identity as 'a matter of "becoming" as well as of "being"' (Hall, 1990: 225). His diaspora theorising was an extension of this perspective, focused on positionings, transformation, *differance* and hybridity:

> The diaspora experience as I intend it here, is defined, not by essence or purity, but by the recognition of a necessary heterogeneity and diversity; by a conception of 'identity' which lives with and through, and not despite, difference; by hybridity. Diaspora identities are those which are constantly producing and reproducing themselves anew, through transformation and difference.
>
> (Hall, 1990: 235)

Gilroy (1993) employed the notion of diaspora to examine sameness, difference and Black diasporic consciousness. He emphasised the hybrid and creole nature of diasporic experience and identity. He was thus able to challenge essentialised understanding of Blackness by employing the notion of diaspora. He associated the latter with central ideas: contingency, indeterminacy and conflict, eschewing notions of origin (Gilroy, 1997: 334). Mercer (1988, 1994), akin to Gilroy, rejected boundedness and revealed the complex nature of Black Britishness, this time focusing on film and diaspora. Appadurai (1991: 191) emphasised how groups were no longer 'tightly territorialized, spatially bounded, historically unselfconscious, or culturally homogenous'. Brah's (1996) work was similarly critical of privileging the point of origin, which ideal-type diaspora theorising had promoted. She instead attempted to reconceptualise 'diaspora space' as different from both the home and the new place. Akin to the notion of 'third space', hybridisation and the 'migrant culture of the "in-between"' (Bhabha, 1994: 27), Brah attempted to rethink diaspora by refusing to confine diaspora to the home or to the new place. She conceptualised it as an 'in-between space', moving it away from gardening tropes of seed, tree and roots. Eschewing home-bounded discussions, Hussain examined the hybridity of British South Asian women, focusing on collective hybrid identities through cultural production (Hussain, 2005). In the same tradition as Gilroy and Hall, although not attempting to theorise diaspora, Joseph-Salisbury (2018) and Tate (2005) discussed hybridity. Their discussions of hybridity centred on resistance and the subversion of the narrow definitions of the category Black, critical (mixed) race theory, and the notion of 'post-racial'.

The hybridity/becoming school was home to the 'roots and routes' debate. Through the works of Clifford (1992, 1997), Gilroy (1993) and Hall (1990), the relationship between place, people and culture was expressed in terms of routes rather than roots (see also Banerjee, 2012). Hall (2006) proposed that instead of roots, we deploy and focus on routes, which he associated with openness. Clifford (1997) showed the intertwining of roots and routes while Gilroy focused attention on displacement and rootedness in the roots and routes axis, and Murji (2008) challenged the assumed dichotomy between roots and routes. Through routes, the hybridity tradition in diaspora thinking prioritised mobility, encounters, traversing of borders, exchanges and hybridity.

Theorisations of diaspora by this tradition sought to examine the lived experiences, contradictions, and heterogeneous and ambivalent expressions of the diasporic condition. The hybridisation and the fight against ethnic absolutism have indeed proven to be successful in terms of shifting our understanding of ethnicity and race. However, I argue that scholars from this tradition were perhaps more successful in employing diaspora in order to challenge essentialist understandings of race and ethnicity, and less focused on diaspora theorising itself. Diaspora ended up as a way to rethink notions of ethnicity and identity. Gilroy (1987: 154), for example, examined 'black cultures within the framework of diaspora as an alternative to the different varieties of absolutism which would confine cultures in "racial", ethnic or national essences'. His later work also continued this theme: 'Diaspora is a valuable idea [as it is] ... an alternative to the metaphysics of "race", nation and bonded culture coded into the body' (1997: 328). Or, as Hall (1990: 222) argues, 'Perhaps instead of thinking of identity as an already accomplished fact, which the new cultural practices then represent, we should think, instead, of identity as a "production", which is never complete, always in process, and always constituted within, not outside, representation.'

However, if all cultures are basically hybrid, there can be little gained in identifying that diasporas are too. If identities are constituted and negotiated, and our cultures are always in a process of hybridisation, then centring our discussions of diaspora on hybridity does not take us very far. In fact, allocating hybridity to diasporic groups might invoke, as Gilroy (1987) also agreed, unwanted notions of 'pureness'. The deployment of the concept of diaspora by the hybridity tradition proved, in my view, to be a means to an end – albeit a valuable one, where essentialist traditions of race and ethnicity and nation were challenged in rigorous and fundamental ways. This tradition was successful in pushing forward the non-essentialist turn in identity research in general, rather than expanding conceptualisations of diaspora *per se*. The concept became a means to de-essentialise identity in general, and race in particular.

Further, even though we are now well-informed that diasporas are not homogeneous, the emphasis put on shifting, ambivalent, situational and fluid identities and on hybridity has not left much room for an understanding of the new battles and challenges faced by diasporas. Nor has diaspora been able to uncover power relations that shape and structure the mixing (Anthias, 1998: 575). Even if these are acknowledged, they can be underplayed through an exclusive focus on hybridity, multiplicity and ambivalence. Issues of cultural hierarchies, exclusion, violence and alienation are not effectively dealt with if diaspora is generally seen as a subjective condition rather than an object of analysis, as pointed out by Anthias (2001: 638), who maintains that 'concerns of hybridity and diaspora are essentially those of culture and consciousness, rather than social inequality and exclusion'. In fact, this cultural turn in diaspora studies has 'watered down the critical possibilities of the concept, focusing inwards on cultural practices and identities at the expense of social, economic and political accounts, and stripping out much of its transformative potential' (Alexander, 2018: 1551). This branch of diaspora theorisation armed us with anti-essentialism, but it did not equip with us with a vocabulary and conceptual framework that would allow us to capture and critically engage with, for example, the backlash that postcolonial diasporas have faced in the West. We know that numerous repetitions of their hybridity unfortunately can do little to understand the hostile responses diasporas currently face. We need to acknowledge, but go further beyond, the hybridity discourse in diaspora theorising if we are to make sense of diasporic conflict and boundary-making in the current global political order.

An overemphasis on shifting and fluid identities, and on the 'infinite process of identity construction' (Gilroy, 1993: 223) can prove to be unhelpful, as it does not allow us to capture transformation and change effectively. In fact, at times 'hybridity offers little more than a stating of the obvious' (Gopal, 2012: 197). If all is in flux and shifting, where does this leave us with identifying – never mind understanding – change and transformation? Akin to this, if contingency and conflict are ever-present, where does this leave us in terms of trying to capture fundamental discords, disputes and clashes? The hybridity tradition can at times blur distinctions to an extent that makes analysis of conflict highly difficult to get a handle on. This is partly because, as Werbner (1997), has identified, there is a paradox between seeing hybridity as both transformative and yet something that is part of the everyday.

Interestingly, 'diaspora as hybridity' has been taken up in cultural studies, and has tended to focus on diasporic subjectivity and diasporic consciousness, producing similar problematic outcomes. Clifford's work on 'diasporic consciousness' (1994), Bhabha's 'third space' and hybrids as cultural brokers (1994) all have rather limited critical insight, often eluding the issue of polarisation, conflict, ghettoisation and backlash to diaspora. While interesting, if the unsettledness, alienation, in-betweenness and homelessness of the diasporic subject are what we mainly focus on, what kind of analytical purchase is diaspora left with? It can 'confirm hierarchy, never its undoing' (Hutnyk, 2005: 99). It is also the case that 'cultural hybridity makes it impossible to displace the hegemonic formation, since the critique of cultural absolutism implied by cultural hybridity also makes it impossible to sustain any subaltern cultural formation' (Sayyid, 2000a: 267; Sayyid, 2000b). It can, at times, conceive of diaspora as a half-way house, or what I regard as 'the tyranny of in-betweenness'.

Interestingly, similar watered-down versions of diaspora, fluidity, diversity, micro-interactions of expatriated minority communities and banal interactions have also found their expression in newer works on migration – for example, through concepts such as 'cosmopolitan sociability' (Glick Schiller, 2014) and 'superdiversity' (Vertovec, 2007). Such concepts, especially their application, equalise difference and promote individualised pluralism, and also offer a greatly reduced potential for empowerment or transformation. Hegemonic formations cannot be challenged and transformed through individualised pluralism alone. While the former problematically juxtaposes cosmopolitanism against multiculturalism (Demir, 2016), the latter – superdiversity – 'contains a powerful sense of social romanticism, creating an illusion of equality in a highly asymmetrical world, particularly in contexts characterized by a search for homogenization' (Makoni, 2012: 193). Vertovec's superdiversity also plays down the importance of racism (Back and Sinha, 2016). It is true that some of the literature on superdiversity recognises new patterns of segregation, provides much-needed examinations of the impact of different migration statuses, and identifies conviviality and enduring relationships (Wessendorf, 2016). It is also true that migrants face challenges irrespective of their colour. Yet so much of the literature on superdiversity and cosmopolitan sociability gets trapped in micro-interactions and individualised plurality. If Bhabha's hybridity constructed 'third space' as a floating cosmopolitan notion, aspects of recent research on cosmopolitan sociability, transnationalism, migration and superdiversity signal a similar narrative. They valorise fluidity, homelessness and, at best, an uncritical diversity. Valorising pluralism without thinking through who holds the upper hand can end up reproducing racialised hierarchies. It cherishes diversity yet disarms the challenge 'the others' bring.

There is also curiously little said in their works on cosmopolitanism and transnationalism about plurality, diversity and multiculturalism being woven into the fabric of European history and society due to colonialism and empire (e.g. Beck, 2011; Delanty, 2011; Glick Schiller et al., 2011; Vertovec, 2007). Discussions of diaspora and superdiversity that ignore empire end up constructing a problematic understanding whereby diversity is conceptualised as something that happened *to* Europe/the West *by* others (newcomers), and only recently. It peddles the view of Europe/the West as untouched and hermetically sealed before post-war migrations, ignoring how European empires were themselves diverse entities. Empire and colonialism are seen as spatially and temporally distant – as something that happened in the past or over there, somewhere else; in either case, they are thought of as having no bearing on Europe/the West today. Hence much work on migration, integration, diversity and cosmopolitanism since the turn of the millennium has consequently ignored colonial legacies and racialised relationships in their analysis, with exceptions – for example, Back and Sinha (2016); Brah (1996, 2018); Favell (forthcoming 2022); Gilroy (2004); Hall (1990, 2007); Hesse (2000); Mayblin (2017).

Additionally, the hybridity tradition has not sufficiently engaged with the fact that there is nothing essentially dynamic, fluid, hybrid or vibrant about migrancy. There is nothing intrinsically liberating in migrancy (Ong and Nonini, 1997: 325). It does not 'necessarily lead to transresistivity or empowerment' (Anthias, 2001: 622). We know that nation-states try to use their 'ethnic kin' when pursuing politics at home and also to gain political leverage. Diaspora can be a 'trope for nostalgia', 'through its naturalising metaphors of roots, soil and kinship' (Soysal, 2000: 13). Yeğenoğlu has been critical, especially about the celebration of migrancy and mobility. She argues (Yeğenoğlu, 2005: 123) that the Anglo-American academic discourse increasingly attributes 'a transformative and resistive power to migrancy, mobility and hybridity'. Chariandy (2006) has also identified that it can overly idealise or even celebrate experiences of dislocation and displacement.

If we are attempting to develop a non-essentialist view of migrancy, the celebration of migrancy, the tired-out association of it with openness and with a celebratory tone is as problematic as its quick dismissal as narrow-minded and nationalistic.[4] What is required is an examination of the processes through which certain migrants and host societies become enablers of open and dynamic engagement; some do not and some other migrant groups actively resist it. The social and political context of the host countries (e.g. openness versus xenophobia), as well as the nature of political consciousness and struggles brought by migrants (e.g. progressive versus conservative) affect the experiences and connections migrants make with their host country, and determine the extent to which their experience can be celebrated as hybrid and open. For these we need to turn to empirical research, and in order to carry out research we need to see diaspora not purely as a subjective condition, but enable its heuristic potential by thinking about how we, as analysts, should employ it.

Last but not least, then, what I have called the 'diaspora as hybridity' school can at times get too fixated about subjectivity at the expense of diaspora as an analytical concept. This can thus prevent newer understandings of diaspora that recognise the urgency of diaspora in understanding and intervening in the world. Anand argues that:

> Rejecting a comprehensive notion of diaspora that includes all types of migrants, I propose confining the term to those collectivities within which individual subjectivity is marked by an ambiguity, a confusion, a productive anxiety, an affective pull from different directions, all of which creates a hyper-awareness and not a permanent sense of regret.
>
> (Anand, 2018: 114)

Diaspora is, of course, about these types of things. But to reduce and confine it to subjective feelings defuses the potency of diaspora, and from a social scientific position exhausts the analytical purchase of diaspora. Diaspora is about exile and collectivity, but it is a normative and political position, a position that problematises coloniality, and is thus closely linked to empire, race and globalisation and the undoings of these in the new home and globally. Diaspora should not be reduced to subjective experiences of longing, homelessness, emotional connections of belonging and of straddling two places at once; it should be much more than these.

Diaspora of diaspora: An unwelcome phenomenon?

As discussed above, the diaspora theorising flourished in the late 1980s and 1990s and the two perspectives discussed above continued to dominate the field. In the following decades, empirical research on diaspora also flourished. On the whole, diaspora theorising since then has situated the discussion and description of diaspora using ideal type conceptualisations or via the hybridity route. While ideal type conceptualisations examined diaspora as a being, the hybridity route underlined hybridity as a becoming. Diaspora was celebrated as and/or accused of these, as shown in Table 1.1.

Table 1.1: Diaspora theorisations

Diaspora as ideal type	Diaspora as hybridity
Being	Becoming
Form	Consciousness, subjectivity
Ethnicity	Fluidity, mobility, flows
Characteristics	Situationist

The use of the concept of diaspora has multiplied since then. Not only the use, but also the different ways in which the concept of diaspora was used, multiplied. It was originally identified by Tölölyan (1996: 8) that diaspora was becoming a 'promiscuously capacious category'. Roger Brubaker (2005) also captured this in his article 'The "Diaspora" Diaspora', in which he criticised the dispersion of the concept, its limitless use, its proliferation and especially its application to many mediums and its meaning being stretched in many directions – in his words, the 'dispersion of the meanings of the term in semantic, conceptual and disciplinary space' (Brubaker, 2005: 1). It seems the dispersion or hybridisation that was welcome for diasporas was not welcome for the concept of diaspora itself.

A student of finitism would, of course, know that meaning determinism is deeply problematic. Finitism, inspired by Wittgenstein's critique of meaning determinism, argues that neither definitions nor the finite number of examples of how to apply a concept can determine how the term will be used in the next instance, or whether it will be the 'correct' application but rather that judgements of correct application are underdetermined except socially. This is because understandings of terms, definitions, rules and analogies are communally sanctioned, including natural-scientific definitions, concepts and methods (Barnes *et al.*, 1996; Bloor, 1997; Kusch, 2002). Diasporisation of the concept of diaspora in a globalised world, its dispersion and proliferation were thus inevitable. Brubaker, in that article, was correct to identify that "If everyone is diasporic, then no one is distinctively so" (Brubaker, 2005: 3). Brubaker's solution to the diasporisation issue was twofold. One was his suggestion to shift diaspora from an 'entity', from a 'bounded group' to 'stances' and 'claims', in line with his well-known 'ethnicity without groupism' perspective. The second was to simplify the key criteria for diaspora:

> As a category of practice, 'diaspora' is used to make claims, to articulate projects, to formulate expectations, to mobilise energies, to appeal to loyalties. It is often a category with a strong normative change. It does not so much describe the world as seek to remake it.
>
> (Brubaker, 2005: 12)

This very interesting position is, of course, an invitation to focus on an examination of how diasporas adopt the diasporic stance and title. Yet there are two problems with this approach. It ends up reducing the use of diaspora to 'user' categories. Besides actor categories, surely the analytical value of diaspora – how and why we, as analysts, should employ it rather than, for example, migration – also needs serious consideration. Additionally, in the very same article, Brubaker (2005) reproduces the Weberian ideal type approach to diaspora through an identification of three core criteria of diaspora: dispersion in space, orientation to a homeland and boundary maintenance. While his call for a focus on 'stances and claims' manages to move away from essentialist constructions of diaspora, the key characteristics approach ends up reintroducing the Weberian ideal type conundrum. It thus faces similar problems: even though boundary-maintenance is one of the key criteria, Brubaker correctly acknowledges its opposite, boundary-erosion, and a few pages down the line argues that, 'Not all discussions of diaspora, to be sure, emphasise boundary-maintenance', revealing the heuristic shortcomings. In addition, the key characteristics of boundary-maintenance, dispersion and homeland orientation also inevitably bring back the 'groupism' from which Brubaker's theorising famously sought to move away.

In the chapters to come, I instead situate diaspora as part of a tradition of decoloniality and provide empirical evidence of this. I deploy it as a stance – but as an analytical stance. I advocate a discussion of diaspora that focuses less on who a diaspora is, or according to what criteria or conditions, than on how diasporas translate and decolonise. I am less interested in ontological issues of being and becoming, but rather seek to focus on epistemology, on how and what diasporas translate and decolonise, and why this matters. I argue that such a conceptualisation and application of diaspora, which make the dislodging of coloniality central to the story and investigation of diasporas, reveal its capacity as a critical concept. Diaspora in this sense enriches understandings of migration rather than running parallel to or against it. By moving from a concern with ontology, or loss and location to translation and decolonisation, I hope to restore and re-establish diaspora as a scholarly concept through also situating it in the intellectual traditions of postcolonialism, decoloniality and the Global South, which allows us to understand and examine diaspora in the context of the traumas of colonialism, nationalism, race, empire, power and violence. The urgency and intellectual contribution of the concept of diaspora best emerges if understood within such contexts, especially *vis-à-vis* dislodging coloniality.

Most often, though, discussions of diaspora are limited to discussions of the nation and nationalism. The critique of 'methodological nationalism' was itself welcome in challenging this in migration studies. However, it is not sufficient, as those who have written critically on methodological nationalism have not made colonialism and empire central to understandings of the nation, nationalism, immigration, transnationalism or post-nationalism. They have challenged nationalism, but not national accounts of the history of nations in the Global North. Transnational accounts have tended to question spatial limitations (of bordered thinking), but not the temporal limitations of nation-centred thinking that ignores colonialism and empire, and their legacies for understanding today. It is no surprise that as such diversity is still seen as something that happened to European nation-states since colonies started coming home from the 1950s onwards rather than heterogeneity and diversity being woven into the history of European societies for centuries as parts of European empires.

If 'diaspora forces us to rethink the rubrics of nation and nationalism' (Braziel and Mannur, 2003: 7), I argue that its use by scholars is long overdue in offering new ways of thinking through the forces of coloniality, decoloniality and globalisation. We need to challenge the often-reproduced categories of citizen versus migrant, domestic versus overseas, national history versus history of empire. Diasporas challenge these and remind us that such divisions are often too simple and inadequate. The works of Gilroy, Hall and Brah were groundbreaking in that regard, and emphasised the legacy of the British empire and diasporic populations. Yet the field of diaspora has now currently come to be 'dominated by single-case studies' (Faist, 2010: 25), focusing either on their relationship to the homeland or the hybrid practices and identities built by diasporas in the new home. While I think such works have made excellent contributions, the field has become rather devoid of critical understandings. We need to explore the interventions that diasporas have made, and continue to make, to the global order in general and the Global North in particular.

The concept of diaspora overlaps with transnationalism and migration, but both the distinction of diaspora and its potential as a critical concept can be revealed and enhanced through translation and decolonisation. For Brubaker (2005: 12), 'As idiom, stance, and claim, diaspora is a way of formulating the identities and loyalties of a population.' I wish to politicise diaspora further. As I will unpack in the rest of this book, diaspora arises as a way of formulating the challenge and resistance to colonisation of expatriate minority communities, their rebellion and transgressiveness – whether these arose in the context of empire, nationalism or globalisation. The notions of 'active or passive diaspora' (Shain and Barth, 2003) or 'dormant diaspora' (Sheffer, 2003) are, in my view, oxymoronic. Diaspora is a special case of migration whereby politicised decolonial subjectivity is associated with mobility. This might risk that I, as an analyst, end up excluding other mobilities under my conceptualisation of diaspora – for example, the privileged migrants who live in Western metropoles, work for transnational companies and reproduce exploitation, also referred to as 'cosmocrats' (Kirwan-Taylor, 2000; Micklethwait and Wooldridge, 2003), or those who reproduce chauvinism or coloniality in the new home. It excludes expat communities who hold and fight to reproduce their privileged status in settler colonies. It would also exclude groups who pursue chauvinistic agendas rather than dislodge nationalist agendas and coloniality (Bhatt, 2000; Thobani, 2019). Reactionary-nationalists who are 'abroad' should not be conceived of as diasporic. As Anand (2018: 115) argues, branding overseas Chinese or Indians or others who privilege 'an essentialist and primordial conception of ethnicity' as a diaspora is problematic. For him, extremists and primordialists should also not be afforded the category of diaspora, as they also essentialise and refuse to negotiate across boundaries. Anthias discusses how those overseas can act as extensions of nationalist discourses and contribute to hyper-nationalisms: Cypriots, Greeks and Turks in London are 'just as likely to provide nationalistic and chauvinistic arguments which serve the perceived political interests of their respective political presentations within the nation state as those who still live in Cyprus' (Anthias, 1998: 567), while newer generations offer solidarities to trans-ethnic alliances. Certain exclusions of mobilisations, stances and activities (rather than ethnic groups) are needed if we are to restore the use of diaspora as an analytic category. All migrant groups and their activities cannot be conceptualised as diasporic without the term losing its explanatory power and critical potential.

At first sight, it looks like I am imposing a limitation on the use of the concept of diaspora. In fact, my conceptualisation of diaspora through translation and decolonisation, as part of a tradition of challenge and resistance, brings a *temporal* dimension to the concept of diaspora and opens new categories of discernment. By temporality I mean that no one group can be deemed as a diaspora eternally. The essentialism and primordialism associated with diaspora arise from it being looked at as an everlasting feature of a group. Such essentialism and primordialism also means that it can be denied, or never afforded to others as easily.

A temporal dimension to understanding diaspora also allows for the recognition that diaspora is not the same as ethnicity or migrancy. Certain migrant groups can become diasporic over time through politics, newer formulations of identity and increasing questioning of coloniality at home or in the new home – for example, how 'migrants' became a Kurdish 'diaspora' in Europe (Demir, 2017a). Such a conceptualisation would also mean that diaspora is not used synonymously to mean ethnicity. Some diasporic groups might share a common ethnic ancestry, but diaspora and ethnicity are not synonymous. For example, Muslim *umma* can be considered as diaspora through a readiness to engage with the political, and through their transnational engagement as Muslim subjectivities (Sayyid, 2000b).

Besides adding a temporal dimension, my conceptualisation of diaspora allows for *heterogeneity*. Within an expatriated group, certain activities, peoples or mobilisations can be seen as diasporic rather than all members and actions being hallmarked with the label. Not everyone within a community is stamped with the same world-view or mobilisation. This is the same for diasporic communities. Those who originate from the same country – even those with the same ethnicity – might have different trajectories and relationships with power, coloniality and globalisation. 'To be Irish in Britain or Australia is not the same as being Irish in America' (Kenny, 2013: 107). Being Senegalese and being Scottish in France are also different experiences, due to race, history, politics and coloniality. Yet one can still recognise, acknowledge and examine the collective action and mobilisation of a diaspora *vis-à-vis* power, coloniality and globalisation without falling into the trap of essentialism. As Ellison (1995: 263) says:

> It is not culture which binds the peoples who are of partially African origin now scattered throughout the world, but an identity of passions. We share a hatred for the alienation forced upon us by Europeans during the process of colonization and empire and we are bound by our common suffering more than by our pigmentation.

Soysal (2000: 2) is right to identify that 'dominant conceptualisations of diaspora presumptively accept the formation of tightly bounded communities and solidarities (on the basis of common cultural and ethnic references) between places of origin and arrival'. There never was a tightly bounded group, community or solidarity, never mind a diaspora. Holistic understandings of any community are problematic. Beliefs and practices of a community can be heterogeneous and contested, and inevitably change over time. If the beliefs of an exiled group become, for example, more tightly knit with the politics of dislodging coloniality at home or in the new home, those members can be conceptualised as constituting a diaspora. Others might decreasingly do so, overridden with xenophobia, chauvinism and nationalist-colonial discourses. Reproducing holistic and eternal understandings of any group, including ethnic groups, is problematic, never mind diasporic groups. Hence the aim should be to jettison holistic and essentialist understandings of diaspora rather than the concept of diaspora itself.

I am unashamedly concerned about diaspora as an analyst category in this book. This focus is worthwhile as long as it corresponds to the empirical reality on the ground and my deployment is congruent with actor behaviour and experiences. Whether a group calls itself diaspora, yet is using it synonymously for migrant, or is deploying it strategically to gain political advantage, or refuses to call itself a diaspora are additional research questions. The purposes to which actors put certain concepts, and how they deploy it or refuse them, require empirical investigation.

Rather than pursuing definitions that problematise or investigate the diasporisation of diaspora by actors, this book aims to expand and make relevant its use for social science and humanities analysts. In summary, diaspora should illuminate a particular aspect of migration if it is to have analytical purchase. My employment of diaspora makes translation and decolonisation central, and places diaspora in the tradition of decoloniality. It risks policing the use of diaspora as an analytical concept, yet it opens up a temporal and non-essentialist understanding of diaspora. It sharpens and makes more precise the use by analysts, yet in arguing that analyst use of diaspora should valorise a particular aspect of migration, it in fact broadens and enriches its scope by distinguishing it from other forms of migration. It also makes the concept of diaspora relevant for understanding the contemporary global age through inviting an identification of how diasporas dislodge coloniality. Indeed, I am troubled by claims that divorce diaspora from colonialism, empire, nationalism, race and ethnicity.

Notes

1 The heuristic potential of ideal types has been challenged by Holmwood and Stewart (1991).

2 I am aware that some of the scholars I group under 'hybridity' did not always deploy the concept themselves – for example, Brah (1996, 2018). Some were at times critical of the essentialist connotations of it, as it can conjure up images of pureness – for example, Gilroy (1987, 1993, 1997, 2004). I locate this group of scholars as the 'hybridity/becoming' group since they focus on becoming and hybridity rather than diaspora as an entity, and because hybridisation is an important aspect of their theorisation. Gilroy deploys Du Bois's concept of double consciousness to convey hybridity as being essential for the diasporic condition even though he rejects pureness, implied through the use of hybridity.

3 It is important to note that Cohen's later work also paid attention to hybridity and becoming through deploying the notion of creolisation (e.g. Cohen and Toninato, 2010; Cohen and Sheringham, 2016).

4 See Chariandy (2006) for a defence of the view that Gilroy's descriptions of diaspora are celebratory.

2

Diaspora as translation

I can't pretend to be you. I don't know your experience. I can't live
life from inside your head. So your living together must depend on
a trade-off, a conversation, a process of translation. Translations are
never total or complete, but they don't leave the elements exactly as
they started.

(Hall, 2007: 151)

This chapter examines diaspora as translation – in other words,
by using the insights of translation studies, I wish to rethink diaspora theorising. This perspective is different from the two central
approaches I identified and critically engaged with in Chapter 1,
namely 'diaspora as an ideal type' and 'diaspora as hybridity'.
These two approaches, one examining 'diaspora as a being' and
the other 'diaspora as a becoming', have enhanced our thinking
of diaspora, yet their ontological focus has hemmed in diaspora
research in particular ways. I wish to move the focus from issues
of being and becoming – for example, what is a diaspora and what
characteristics do diasporas have? – to discussions of translation
and decolonisation, and thereby expand our knowledge, thinking
and understanding of diaspora. What concerns me is a central epistemological issue of what intervention diaspora research can and
should make to global understandings. A focus on the dynamics
of diaspora as translation and diaspora as decolonisation, I argue,
can expand thinking and understanding of diaspora within the
current dynamics of our globalised world. Translation is not just
a useful metaphor for understanding the movement and struggles
of diasporas; more importantly, translation studies has much
insight to offer, from which we can learn, apply and extend our
understandings in diaspora studies. Through this new perspective,
which I call 'diaspora as translation', along with Chapter 3 on

'diaspora as decolonisation', I propose to provide not only a new and productive way of conceptualising diaspora but also provide a useful positive heuristic device for investigating diasporas.

Translation has, of course, long been a source of inspiration and also of concern for social and critical theorists, and for post-colonial thinkers. Spivak (2004), for example, theorises translation in the context of submission and understanding rather than equivalence. Locating translation in inequality in translation, Spivak (2004) also calls for reflexivity in translation and notes its political consequences. Another postcolonial scholar, Bhabha (1994), focuses on cultural translators as located in in-between spaces, creating hybrid visions and perspectives. Derrida's theorising has been radical, destabilising the notion of origin that traditionally has been central to translation. He has also challenged the translatable/untranslatable dichotomy, arguing that a text simultaneously involves both untranslatability and translatability. While no language or culture can be totally subsumed and fully represented in another, languages (and peoples) often reach beyond their own linguistic and cultural boundaries (Derrida, 1979; Foran, 2011). For Ricoeur (2006), another important scholar of translation, the translation problematic has to be viewed not from the prism of translatability/untranslatability, but rather from the perspective of faithfulness and betrayal. Moreover, for him, there is a further dimension and difference which needs unpacking: translation between people and texts. Ricoeur argues that the dialogical situation between peoples is different from the engagement with, and translation of, a written text. While the former can potentially share a common situation with its interlocutor, tailor the messages to the hearer and ask for clarifications, engagements with texts are always open, as 'there is always more than one way of construing a text' (Ricoeur, 2006).

Benjamin's (1968) reading of translation as a tangent that touches the source yet follows its own path is perhaps one of the best-known interventions in terms of unpacking the 'tense' relationship between the source text, translator and translation, revealing translation's promise but also its close link to the source. While the translator touches the original, as the tangent touches the circle, and is thus inextricably tied to the source text, they do so only at one point, meaning the path is open and undetermined. He also uses the image of a shattered vessel in order to communicate how translation recreates using fragments of meaning and language, signalling transition, indeterminacy and rewriting involved in translation.[1] Following Benjamin, yet taking his arguments further via anthropology, translation has also been a source of concern for Asad's engagement with the discipline of anthropology and for his discussions of Eurocentrism (1986, 1995). Asad (1986: 157) argues that translators should concern themselves with testing the tolerance of their own language and culture, dissecting, reshaping and rewriting them rather than searching for equivalence. More recently Bielsa's (2016) work on translation has explored the close relationship between globalisation and translation.

Translation has thus been an inspiration for social theory, and its central insights have informed and expanded understandings of authenticity, in-betweenness, untranslatability and hybridity. I argue that translation – that is, the attempt to achieve understanding between two languages and cultures – is a suitable metaphor for explaining the asymmetry, frictions, retelling and relationships inherent in the diasporic condition. As mediators, diasporas act as agents who connect, translate, shift and move across linguistic and cultural zones. They are the archetypal intermediaries and translators – for example, to the host community, back to homeland, or to the second generation. They put cultures, identities and languages, and new ideologies, into circulation. They are translators of identities and cultures brought from home. They also often resist existing norms and challenge power relations in their translations. Moreover, they can facilitate communication and interaction but also act as gatekeepers, or advocate incommensurability between the home and the host. Theorists of diaspora have highlighted diasporic hybridity, yet we need to recognise that diasporas also erase, domesticate and rewrite.

A focus on translation also helps to place untranslatability, hierarchy and difficulties of cultural interaction at the centre of our discussions of diaspora and thus of global conversations. It can complicate our understanding of diaspora. Talal Asad's work (e.g. Asad, 1986), alongside works by Siegel (1993), Fabian (1986) and Robinson (1997) acknowledge that translation was central to anthropology and to regimes of colonial power, as well as to understanding current hierarchies. If we think back, it is partly through a critical engagement with language and incommensurability that anthropology was transformed from a 'Victorian' discipline to a critical one, and started questioning the taken for granted nature of the debates around 'primitives' and 'moderns'. As translation became central to the concerns of anthropologists, difficulties of conveying ideas from one culture to another came to be acknowledged and examined rather than assumed as easily surmountable. Naïve conceptualisations in anthropology were challenged via a focus on language and translatability.

If critical anthropologists paid attention to translation and language in order to reveal hierarchies and problems to do with communication, incommensurability and cultural interaction arising from European expansion and colonisation, my aim is to turn the tables on this approach and instead look at flows (of peoples and cultures) going to the Global North from the Global South as diasporas. Making translation central to our understanding of diaspora can help us to rethink diaspora, and place it at the centre of our understanding of modernity, globalisation and politics today. Diaspora is not just associated with the movement of 'others' to Europe. Diasporas also 'speak back' to the metropole directly. They are the Global South in the Global North, translating and talking 'back' to the Global North. We can thus conceptualise diaspora from this new perspective – that is, as one of the central agents working towards the decolonisation of the North.

Another reason for conceptualising diaspora as translation is that it encapsulates how diasporas can be a source of liberation and progress. This is different from an association of diaspora and migrancy with essential states of openness and positivity. Decolonisation is not openness: diasporas can restrict and put a lid on what is translated, how is it translated and what is forgotten or remembered from the home. How and what kind of stories diasporas revive, the kinds of political struggles they bring, what they revive or create, and how the translations of diasporas are met with by the 'hosts' need a close examination. We can examine whether different types of diasporic translation entrench incommensurabilities. An examination of the translational activities of a diaspora can help reveal the extent to which diaspora is a possible agent of resistance and decolonisation. It can help assess enablers of such interventions, and identify impediments to them. Accommodating and domesticating translations that run away from decolonisation and foreignisations can in fact produce problematic outcomes by valorising difference yet glossing over the difference that difference should make. Discussions of translation *vis-à-vis* migration are, of course, not new within the field of translation studies. Cronin (2003, 2006) and Polezzi (2012) have already made useful observations on the relationship between migration, globalisation and translation. Cronin (2006: 52), for example, discusses the various translational strategies immigrants may adopt in their new home: they may seek 'translational assimilation' or 'translational accommodation'. While the former is aimed at erasing the home, the latter prioritises translation so migrants can maintain their languages of origin. Additionally, Polezzi (2012) has highlighted that migrants employ translation for accommodation but also for resistance. My aim in this chapter is to build on such work, but most importantly to deploy the many insights and concepts of translation studies in order to enrich diaspora studies. Translation studies has much to offer to the field of migration in general, and diaspora in particular. For this, we need to move past traditional conceptions of translation and pay attention to the many insights of the field of translation studies.

Translation studies and diaspora

As I discussed above, translation itself is a good metaphor for understanding diasporas and transnationalism, but we should not restrict ourselves just to that. Translation studies offers many conceptual tools and enrichment for understanding and researching diasporas, as discussed below. Translation studies emerged out of the field of applied linguistics, and the bulk of early work in translation studies focused on textual issues – for example, examining issues to do with fidelity, equivalence, semantics and meaning transfer, exposing intricacies of translation and interpretation. The field has expanded, with cultural and sociological approaches to translation becoming popular, examining translation in a social context. Other new approaches to translation developed in time – for example, feminist (Simon, 1996) and postcolonial stances (Cheyfitz, 1991; Niranjana, 1992; Rafael, 1993; Robinson, 1997;

Spivak, 2004), and critical approaches (Asad, 1986, 1995; Berman, 2004; Tymoczko and Gentzler, 2002; Tymoczko, 2007; Venuti, 1992, 1995). These new approaches conceived the relationship between source and target not as one of equals, but rather as a hierarchy, and aimed to reveal the way in which translation takes place in a social context of domination and potentially as a site of liberation. Translation needed to be thought of as a point of contact between languages and people holding differing powers (Tymoczko and Gentzler, 2002).

Such new approaches also signalled a shift from linguistic concerns to the social and cultural context in which translation takes place. The shift was coined as the 'cultural turn' by Snell-Hornby (1988) and by Bassnett and Lefevere (1998). They identified and examined the shift in emphasis to issues such as

> how a text is selected for translation, for example, what role the translator plays in that selection, what role an editor, publisher or patron plays, what criteria determine the strategies that will be employed by the translator, how a text might be received in the target system. For a translation always takes place in a continuum, never in a void, and there are all kinds of textual and extratextual constraints upon the translator.
>
> (Bassnett, 1998a: 123)

This cultural turn significantly shaped the discipline of translation studies from the 1990s onwards: 'The unit of translation was no longer a word or a sentence or a paragraph or a page or even a text, but indeed the whole language and culture in which that text was constituted' (Trivedi, 2005). It freed translation studies from having to focus solely on language. There are, of course, affinities between the cultural turn in translation studies and the rise of cultural studies. As Trivedi (2005) notes, the liberation of translation from linguistics followed another turn whereby cultural studies itself went through a translation turn as identified in the title of the chapter 'The Translation Turn in Cultural Studies' by Bassnett and Lefevere (1998).

What has come to be referred to as the sociological turn also contributed to the shift in the focus from linguistic concerns, this time to the role of the translator. The sociological turn in translation studies has, on the whole, been shaped by the insights of Pierre Bourdieu. It uses his concepts of 'field' and 'habitus' to uncover the role of the translator. Much of the contribution of such works has been to translation studies rather than to sociology. The 'translation sociology' associated with actor-network theory of Callon and Latour also advocates the study of translation (e.g. Callon, 1984). The approach focuses on an articulation of social relations as 'traceable associations'. The main contribution here is to sociology, on developing an understanding of how people speaking for others accrue power through making themselves central and indispensable.

What is most important for my argument is that, through the various 'turns' and the works of Lawrence Venuti, Antoine Berman, Gayatri Spivak, Tejaswini Niranjana and Douglas Robinson, among others, power came to be situated at the centre of the practice of translation. This interest in the relationship between power and translation was coined 'the power turn' in cultural studies by Tymoczko and Gentzler (2002). Issues of agency, change, dominance, cultural assertion, activism, resistance, discourse structures and censorship came to be examined and studied. Translation studies moved from a 'pure' interest in word-for-word or sense-for-sense translation, to a more complex context where translation studies scholars have increasingly become interested in uncovering power and social belief systems, including paying attention to the culture, society and context in which translations take place. New approaches in translation studies have also developed in fields such as anthropology, sociology and (colonial) history. Recently in science and technology studies, and in health sciences, translation has emerged as a core interest. The use of the term 'bench to bedside', which describes the transformation of bioscience into therapeutic practice, became a focal issue as early as 1985 (Merz, 1985; Zerhouni, 2005), while issues of communication, belief and knowledge between scientists, and also between social workers, have been conceived as related to translation (Demir and Murtagh, 2013; Mitchell and Demir, 2021; Murtagh et al., 2011). So is there a way in which we can borrow insights from translation studies to further our understanding of diaspora?

The lure of translation for diaspora

Translating identity, culture and practice, and relating these to others' language and culture – including to back home – are some of the central concerns of diasporas. Both translation and diaspora are about communication and interaction across borders; they are also about interaction across differences and hierarchies. Siegel (1993: 3) argues that, 'Translation and hierarchy are intimately intertwined.' Diaspora is about seeing difference, but then also about interacting given those differences and hierarchies – be they linguistic, cultural or ethno-political. Here I am going beyond the idea of language being seen simply as a barrier to translation and communication. Just as we can acknowledge the limits of language, yet see that translation and communication happen despite the linguistic challenges, we need to extend our understanding of diaspora and see it as a site of interaction, convergence and hybridity, but also of hierarchy, resistance and opposition.

Diaspora as rewriting and transformation

According to Lefevere (1992: 9), a leading scholar of translation studies, translation is a form of rewriting. This is because translation ends up manipulating the original, shaping it in the politics, ideology and world-view of the translator, and it crafts the original for the target culture. Such manipulations can be culturally mediated or ideologically driven, but translators end up rewriting and thus transforming the 'original'.

Even though Lefevere's (1992) view of translation as rewriting had antecedents, his unpacking of the implications of what that means has shifted the field significantly. His work challenges the view of translators as neutral mediators, simply transferring meaning. He brings to our attention the insufficient due regard given to the way translators 'rewrite'. For him, translation is far from being a neutral activity and his view is that all translations in fact distort the original. Lefevere's view of translation as rewriting follows the Wittgensteinian argument that language is a social practice, and that those who speak it craft and extend it, at times according to the culture of the target. If each use and application of a concept is an extension, so is the translation of each new concept. In this sense,

Lefevere's ideas take forward what Benjamin (1968) examines by tasking the translator with rewriting, renewal and transformation. Translation as rewriting also points us towards the argument that translation is in fact always a site of 'gain and discovery' (Bassnett and Trivedi, 1999: 4). Moreover, and perhaps most importantly, translation does not just subvert the original; it goes further and challenges the futility of our craving for authenticity – a salient point for diaspora studies.

Translation studies has thus brought to our attention the fact that many of us today read works not in their originals but in their rewritings. Translations of identities and cultures brought from home are also forms of rewriting and transformation. First, when diasporas translate identity and struggles, their translations of the home should be seen as sites of 'gain and discovery', as something that is far from a simple transfer of meaning and culture. Unpacking how this occurs opens new avenues of research in diaspora studies. Second, this perspective reminds us that diasporas are not creating equivalences with identities, cultures and ideologies formed at home – indeed, far from it, we should see transfer of meaning, fidelity and transformations in need of being revealed through empirical investigations. Third, the translation of identity, self and culture in which diasporas engage is an important type of rewriting that needs to be seen as culturally mediated and ideologically driven. Diasporas, as translators, become authors and the ways in which they shape meaning and identity need to be interrogated closely. Just as the translator has power and uses judgement to assess differences, disparities and asymmetries, diasporas can introduce newness, alter meaning, distort the home. They also need to deal with cultural gaps. Fourth, the translation of identity in which diasporas engage is also shaped by the receiving culture. Rewriting is done for a particular audience, not in a vacuum. Diasporas craft identity for the target audience; the social and political context of the receiving culture, especially its racial and power hierarchies, is indirectly an author in these rewritings. The extent to which receiving cultures and states shape translations of diasporas needs unpacking.

The perspective of diaspora as rewriting also challenges the pointless craving for authenticity and the binary world-view into which the field of diaspora studies at times traps itself. In diaspora studies, there is a tendency to tie ourselves in the dichotomies of home and away, of authenticity and change, of origins and arrivals, nationalism and post-nationalism. The point, of course, is not that we stop using these concepts but rather that we change and challenge our static understandings of them. Such problems are dealt with in interesting ways in translation studies, as they have been thinking about, but also beyond, the problems of 'originality and authenticity, of power and ownership, of dominance and subservience' (Bassnett, 1998b: 27). When it comes to diasporas, there is also the added complexity that the original – in this case, the homeland – is not fixed in time and space. The original – that is, the home – is in constant change, renewal and modification as well. Additionally, the translations in which diasporas engage are complex due to the negotiations with the home as well as interactions with the target audience manoeuvring and shaping how the translation occurs. The translations of ethno-political identities in which diasporas engage should thus be seen and traced as shaping, among other things, what the translated end product will be, as having made interventions into what the original is/was and in relation to the changing homeland. By examining such translational practices of diasporas, we can unpack the creative ways in which they carry out renewal, rewriting, erasure and transformation, and explore how they deal with issues of authenticity. If translation studies has taught us that translation is to be understood by its difference from the original, the field of diaspora studies needs to consider and make much more of the notion that diaspora is a form of rewriting and transformation, and move away from 'the tyranny of in-betweenness' that underpins much of the thinking in the field.

Diaspora as erasure and exclusion

A second way in which this chapter attempts to rethink diaspora through translation is by making erasure and exclusion central to our understanding of diaspora. Translation is not only a site of gain, discovery and reward, but also of erasure, exclusion and violence. Violent and imperialistic metaphors have dominated theories and conceptualisations of translation. For example, cannibalism has been used as a metaphor for the ways in which a language and culture of one group is consumed in the language and culture of another (Viera, 1999). St Jerome, in a similar vein, has conceptualised the source language as a prisoner, marched into another country (target language) by its conqueror, the translator (Robinson, 1997).

Beyond metaphors, translation has been a necessity for colonisation. As Venuti (2002: 158) has argued, 'The colonization of the Americas, Asia, and Africa could not have occurred without interpreters, both native and colonial, nor without the translations of effective texts, religious, legal, educational.' The colonisers have needed it to impose their power and the colonised have had to understand the new rulers and therefore have needed it to formulate and continue the relationship with their new masters. Translators have allowed imperial conquerors to communicate with, convert and dominate the colonised. Colonisation has made translation a necessity. Ironically, in certain cases it made translation impossible: The Act for the English Order, Habit and Language (1537) required the Irish to adopt the English language (as well as behaviour and dress). Speaking in Irish and its translation effectively became associated with treason (Williams, 2013: 57).

The cultural and political turn in translation studies has enabled the exposition of asymmetries and domination produced and reproduced via translation. The role of translation in colonialism and domination has been examined by various scholars of both translation and empire. Robinson's (1997: 10) seminal work put colonialism at the heart of translation: 'translation has always been an indispensable channel of imperial conquest and occupation'. Niranjana (1992) and Cheyfitz (1991) have shown the role played by translation for empire, focusing on the ways in which ethnographic translation has been a central vehicle for domination. While Niranjana's case has been the nineteenth-century translation of India by the British empire, the work of Cheyfitz has been the sixteenth- and seventeenth-century translation of the New World by Europe. Niranjana has critically examined the 'civilising' role of the British in India. The British parliamentarian Thomas Macaulay, who was appointed president of the Committee for Public Instruction in 1835, made language instruction and the instruction of translators in India central. His own writings show the link between translation, domination and empire: 'We must at present do our best to form a class who may be interpreters between us and the millions whom we govern; a class of persons, Indian in blood and colour, but English in taste, in opinions, in morals and in intellect' (Macaulay, 1995: 428–30). Critical of such 'civilising' missions, Niranjana (1992: 173) has instead called for 'a practice of translation that is speculative, provisional and interventionist', which would focus attention on difference and resist erasure. Rafael (1993) has examined the role of translation and identified the misconnections and mistranslations in the Spanish conversion of the Tagalogs in the Philippines, and concluded that for the Spanish the aim of translation was to make the culture accessible for intervention – be it divine or imperial. Translation was also a tool for resisting colonisation. Irish translators resisted British colonisation in their translations (Tymoczko, 1999). Translation continued to be fraught in Ireland also 'after' independence (Cronin, 1996). As is beautifully explored in Brian Friel's (1981) play *Translations*, translation has been a channel of colonisation.

Translations of scholarly work have paved the way for colonisers to dominate. For example, Abdelmajid Hannoum (2003) discusses this in relation to how translations of Ibn Khaldûn, the fourteenth-century North African scholar, by William de Slane were instrumental in the colonisation of Algeria. The translation of Khaldûn's history of Arabs and Berbers in the Maghreb was a central source of knowledge of North Africa for the French colonisers at the time, but 'has become since then the source of French knowledge of North Africa' (Hannoum, 2003: 61). Hannoum traces the way this knowledge was 'converted' into a useful tool for colonial domination. Moreover, colonisation and imperialism have written a blank cheque for making crude ethnocentric judgements about 'others'. The Orientalised and racialised stereotypes expressed in the translations by colonial regimes, intellectuals and artists have been studied by translation scholars, and literary and cultural studies scholars. Said's (1978) book *Orientalism* has shown how, in the modern imperial age, the Europeans viewed non-Europeans through distorting, flawed lenses, which has come to shape our understanding of, and interaction with, the Middle East. Such lenses have not only constituted the East, but also the idea of the West.

Furthermore, such translations by colonisers can even shape how the colonised continue to perceive and understand themselves and their history today. Niranjana's (1992) discussion of the way Indians learnt about their historical and cultural texts in English – that is, via the translations of the original Indian-language texts into English by the East India Company (the colonial government) – is pertinent:

> European translations of Indian texts prepared for a Western audience provided the 'educated' Indian with a whole range of Orientalist images. Even when the Anglicized Indian spoke a language other than English, 'he' would have preferred, because of the symbolic power conveyed by English, to gain access to his own past through the translations and histories circulating through colonial discourse.
>
> (Niranjana, 1992: 31)

Niranjana's work unpacks the relationship between historians, colonial administrators and translators in order to examine the role of translation in colonisation. For her, translation became the site through which unequal relationships were reproduced. Such an approach thus demonstrated the naïve way in which translation had typically been understood – that is, as transparent and objective. Yet translation was instrumental in locking cultures in a certain place and time, in freezing 'others' as unchanging and eternal.

The role of translation can be traced through to postcolonial times. The asymmetries enabled and the violence perpetuated by translation do not just exist in history. Contemporary translation practices help to reproduce hierarchies and asymmetries between peoples and spaces, similar to those that supported colonialism. Never mind the 'trade deficit' between the core and the periphery in terms of how little is translated into English (or into European languages from non-European ones), translation can reproduce inequalities, exclusions and asymmetries when translators transfer meaning or map information and language from one language to another. Bielsa and Bassnett (2009: 11), for example, illustrate this through a focus on international news agencies, and through unpacking the ways in which the media translate news from other countries, 'moulding the news material'.

Postcolonial translation studies has considered translation in contexts that were dominated by radical linguistic and cultural differences accompanied by asymmetric power relations. Richard

Jacquemond (1992) provides a general scheme of translational inequalities, as outlined by Robinson (1997: 31):

1. A dominated culture will invariably translate far more of a hegemonic culture than the latter will of the former.
2. When a hegemonic culture does translate works produced by the dominated culture, those works will be perceived and presented as difficult, mysterious, inscrutable, esoteric and in need of a small cadre of intellectuals to interpret them, while a dominated culture will translate a hegemonic culture's works accessibly for the masses.
3. A hegemonic culture will only translate those works by authors in a dominated culture that fit the former's preconceived notions of the latter.
4. Authors in a dominated culture who dream of reaching a large audience will tend to write for translation into a hegemonic language, and this will require some degree of compliance with stereotypes.

Translation can thus install stereotypes of the periphery in the core, and it can fix those stereotypes of the periphery in the language and mind of the periphery itself. Translation can also carry the violence and erasures to other cultures and languages through subsequent translations into other languages. Fowler (1992) has shown how American translators and publishers shaped and created Japanese stereotypes through their translations of Japanese fiction. Diverging 'all too widely from the reality of contemporary Japan' (Fowler, 1992: 3), certain stereotypes inscribed in their translations were then picked up and translated into, and thus reproduced in, other subsequent languages. According to Fowler (1992: 3), these translations were central to the creation of certain stereotypes of Japan in many other cultures and languages. Aijaz Ahmad (1992) has identified a similar 'journey' for Latin American fiction. Latin American texts arrive in India via US and British publishers, and critical commentators. Such 'translations affect not simply the ways in which non-Western cultures are perceived and discussed in the "First World", but also how they are subsequently recuperated in various parts of the "Third World"' (Dingwaney, 1995: 6).

Inspired by such insight from translation studies, I argue that diasporas, as translators of culture, identity and struggles, have the potential to erase, omit and exclude. 'There is ordinarily no full equivalence through translation,' says Susan Bassnett-MacGuire (1991: 14). We know from studies of translation and incommensurability that even in science, where objectivity and neutrality are seen as key, full translation and one-to-one mapping of concepts and ideas across scientific traditions, communities and languages is not possible (Kuhn, 1996; Favretti et al., 1999). It is inevitable that the translations of culture and identity in which diasporas engage will include omissions and exclusions.

We can examine diasporas through a rewriting of translational inequalities into diasporic experience that Jacquemond (1992) and Robinson (1997) have suggested. Below, I take their categorisation and apply it to diasporas – albeit using the word 'translation' to refer to the ways in which diasporas revive and retell ethno-political identity. I present these as propositions to be investigated rather than as assumptions:

1. A dominated[2] diaspora will invariably translate far less into the hegemonic host than the latter will into the former.
2. When a hegemonic host ends up engaging and translating the culture and identity of the dominated diaspora, the culture and language will be perceived and presented as difficult, mysterious, inscrutable, esoteric and in need of a small cadre of intellectuals to interpret it, while a dominated diaspora will be expected to translate a hegemonic host accessibly for the masses.
3. A hegemonic host will usually translate those ideas, cultures and practices of a dominated diaspora that fit the former's preconceived notions of the latter.
4. Those in diasporas who dream of reaching large audiences in the host country will tend to appeal to the hegemonic culture, and this will require some degree of compliance with existing stereotypes.

Conceiving of diaspora as a process of translation has an immense heuristic potential and can allow us to further explore the empirical validity of such propositions alongside questions that diaspora scholars have asked, such as: 'Who travels when, and under what circumstances? What socio-economic, political and cultural conditions mark the trajectories of these journeys? What regimes of power inscribe the formation of a specific diaspora?' (Brah, 1996: 182). Such important questions can be complicated further through a focus on translation of identity. They can turn our attention to uncovering what diasporas omit consciously as well as unconsciously. They can also help us to trace the erasures and exclusions in the translations of ethno-political or cultural identity. Such a focus can push us to investigate omissions in the translation of the home to the new host, and of the home to new audiences found in diaspora – for example, to other diasporic communities in disadvantaged neighbourhoods of Europe. Erasures do not need to be treated with suspicion: less can be more for the stories diasporas tell and the mobilisations in which they engage. More importantly, such questions do not just examine the diasporic community at hand, but also pay close attention to the hegemonic host, how the reception and politics of the hegemonic host shape what diasporas are able and willing to tell, how they tell, and what is left out and why. In addition, they can drive an examination of what knowledges diasporas incite but also hide from their second (and further) generations. In summary, the conceptualisation of diaspora as translation can have heuristic outcomes by motivating researchers to focus on the uncovering of how and why diasporas withhold stories from the hosts, their newer generations or those at home. We can expose the leaks as well as the resistance to leaks by diasporas. Last but not least, the erasures and exclusions of diasporas can be examined not just by looking at what they choose to omit, but by investigating the knowledges, identities and histories they repeat and incite.

Notions of erasure and exclusion, of course, raise the perennial question of authenticity that I began to discuss earlier. What is the authentic identity, culture or home that diasporas are supposed to betray? The notion of diaspora at first sight requires an assessment of authentic links with the home, just as manipulation, fidelity and betrayal have been the concerns of translation studies. A rudimentary and simple understanding of diaspora craves authenticity. Yet, as I discussed above, diaspora – just like translation – destabilises existing notions of both origin and telos. Craving or searching for authenticity *vis-à-vis* diaspora is also dangerous. It can end up constructing the home as eternal and unchanging – static similar to what Niranjana (1992) identified with regard to the role of translation in coloniality. By making translation central to diaspora, my aim is not to see or measure whether diasporas are faithful to the homeland or to the new home; rather, it is to recognise that diasporas reinforce but also simultaneously transform and police diasporic culture and identity. As researchers, we do not have to fuss over authenticity *per se*, but instead should unpack the types of authenticity and fidelity to which diasporas, as social actors, give precedence.

Diaspora as tension between foreignisation and domestication

Translation is not only a process of gain and reward, but can shut down dialogue, cross-breeding and learning. This is because translation can be ethnocentric and end up reproducing stereo-types and prejudice. Such ethnocentric aspects of translation were picked up and discussed by scholars of translation. Antoine Berman (1992: 5) emphasised how translation 'generally under the guise of transmissibility carries out a systematic negation of the strangeness of the foreign work'. Lawrence Venuti (1995) argued that strangeness of texts is often erased and made invisible in Anglo-American translations into English. This is because the role of an ideal translator was understood to be to make the translated text read fluently. Venuti (1995) provided plenty of examples of how invisibility and erasure were achieved through what he called 'domesticating' the foreign text, making them read smoothly, thus rewriting it in the culture and world-view of the receiving cul-ture, in line with what Anglo-American publishers and reviewers demanded. The translator would be invisible, giving the impres-sion that it was written in the translated language – the target lan-guage. Others simply were not translated into European languages. While the works of Nobel Laureate Naguib Mahfouz, which sat-isfied European visions of Egyptian society, were translated, his later works, which did not meet Western expectations, were not (Jacquemond, 1992). Domesticating strategies erase the difference of the foreign text and pander to readers' expectations, prejudices and world-views. The disruptions and challenges the peripheral could bring to the receiving dominant language and culture are not always materialised. According to Venuti (1995: 12), British and American publishing

> has reaped the financial benefits of successfully imposing Anglo-
> American cultural values on a vast foreign readership, while

producing cultures in the United Kingdom and the United States that are aggressively monolingual, unreceptive to the foreign, accustomed to fluent translations that invisibly inscribe foreign texts with English-language values and provide readers with the narcissistic experience of recognizing their own culture in a cultural other.

Berman and Venuti both argued against domestication, fluency and invisibility. They called for the reader to be foreignised, made aware of the fact that they were reading a translated text (Berman, 1992; Venuti, 1992, 1995). Venuti and Berman's approaches were influenced by what is known as the Schleiermacher model of translation in its demand for foreignising. Schleiermacher (1768–1834) was himself influenced by the Romantic tradition and hermeneutics, and argued that translations 'into German should read and sound different' and that 'the alterity of the source text' should not be lost but preserved (Bassnett and Lefevere, 1998: 8). Schleiermacher's concepts of alienating and naturalising were then taken up by Venuti as foreignisation and domestication, and further elaborated. Venuti contrasted his 'foreignising translation' with 'domesticating translation'. While domestication appropriates one in the language of the other, foreignisation keeps the strangeness of the original. Translation through foreignisation refuses erasure through smoothing; instead, it invites the core and periphery languages and cultures to interact and engage. It refuses assimilative translation. This is not to say that a foreignising strategy would demand a word-for-word translation. As O'Neill (2011: 135) highlights:

> Word-for-word translation is often used as a part of a foreignizing strategy, but is not in itself foreignizing. Foreignizing strategies are, as are domesticating ones, loaded with socio-cultural and political power struggles and the subjectivity that comes with such an approach far surpasses that of an individual translator.

Others have also advocated a foreignising strategy – albeit using different names and techniques. Niranjana's understanding of translation shows how the reception of the original was constituted by power relations and especially, as I discussed above, through the colonial project. She argued for retranslation whereby colonised peoples translated their texts so the cultural traces of the coloniser were eradicated (Niranjana, 1992). Karamcheti, on the other hand, argued for opaque translation – for example, leaving aboriginal names of trees and fauna in order to remind the reader that they were reading a translation (1995: 188). Akin to this, Gentzler (2008) praised 'partial translation' and 'mistranslation', while Tymoczko (2007) considered the 'compensation approach' – that is, how translators could make up for difference or ignorance by offering explanations and background. White (1995: 38) took it much further and defended 'the virtue of not understanding', and of turning 'moments of "not understanding" into "spaces for learning"':

> to create a seemingly effortless text, would be to erase the reality of the other language – the possibilities for life and feeling it offers, the experiences of those who live on its terms – which would be an ethical as well as aesthetic wrong, a violation of the translator's duty of fidelity to the original. This is especially so where speakers of the other language are politically subordinate to those to whom the translation is addressed.
>
> (White, 1995: 333–4)

Foreignisation strategies have, of course, been promoted and carried out by feminist translators since the 1980s. Louise von Flotow (1991), for example, identified four feminist strategies: footnoting, supplementing, prefacing and hijacking. These strategies abused fidelity in order to make the feminine visible. They refused to collude with patriarchal language, avoided male forms, injected female pronouns, hijacked through radical rewritings and challenged their writers:

> By making the feminine seen and heard in her translation, de Lotbinière-Harwood deliberately contravenes conventional translation practice of being see-through and silent. Her strategies include using the word Québécois-e-s wherever the generic Québécois occurred in the original — a source-language feminization tactic which she explains in her preface. She avoids other male generic terms in English although they appear in French, i.e. "la victoire de l'homme" becomes "our victory … over the elements"; she puts the female element first in expressions like "women and men," "her or his," and uses inverted quotation marks to emphasize some of the absurdities of conventional English, for example, the reference to women as "masters" of the kitchen. De Lotbinière-Harwood has in fact "hijacked" the text, appropriated it, made it her own to reflect her political intentions.
>
> (Flotow, 1991: 79)

Feminist scholars not only 'womanhandled' texts, but also questioned naïve forms of universalism:

> Divorcing itself from the unrealizable ideals of universal humanism, translation must work today through new logics of communication, through new configurations of commonality. Feminist interventions into translation have served to highlight the fact that cultural transmission is undertaken from *partial* (and not universal) perspectives, from constantly evolving cultural *positions*.
>
> (Simon, 1996: 166 emphasis original)

Domestication and foreignising are thus forms of intervention. The former makes the translated text familiar, understandable, digestible and able to be read fluently. But it does injustice to the foreign text, as it smooths over the edges, and takes the foreignness away. In some sense, we can compare this domestication role to the way anthropologists have been tasked with making sense of the foreign and rendering the foreign in the world-view of the anthropologists' culture or in their academic discourses. However, as Asad (1995) has brought to our attention in his analysis of cultural translation, uncovering the implicit meanings of subordinate societies should carry with it an understanding of the authority carried by anthropologists, including the violence involved in making other cultures translated ethnocentrically via anthropology:

> The process of translating always involves discrimination, interpretation, appraisal and selection. It calls for a constant awareness of the limits and possibilities of translating adequately from one language to another. And, of course, one translates texts for a variety of purposes, some benign and some hostile to the producers of the original texts. But none of this implies that the practice of translation can't be distinguished from the practice of critique.
>
> (Asad, 1995: 326)

Ricoeur's (2006, 2007) discussions of 'linguistic hospitality' also have much in common with those who seek foreignisation and resist erasure in translation. Ricoeur abandons the idea of perfect translation and calls for linguistic hospitality – that is, for translation to host the other language in one's own. For him, 'the pleasure of dwelling in the other's language is balanced by the pleasure of receiving the foreign word at home' (Ricoeur, 2006: 10). Moreover, his works deal with translation in the context of difference and the diversity of cultures and languages, and thus with self-transformation: it is 'as much about recognizing the limits of our own understanding as it is about overcoming them' (Maitland, 2017: 8). Those in the host society re-learn themselves and understand themselves better – they discover the limits as well as the richness of their own culture and language. Translation, just like being in diaspora, makes those limits vivid and immediate. It is no coincidence that Riceour has seen linguistic hospitality as a model for other forms of hospitality.

This last point neatly brings us to the issue with which we began – that is, what kind of insights can we draw for diaspora studies? Diaspora, like translation, can foreignise as well as domesticate. It can transport difference or erase it, and its reception in the host is constituted by power relations in the home and the new place. Just as those whose native language is not English constantly translate themselves into dominant languages in order to communicate (Cronin, 2003: 60), diasporic groups have to translate their identity struggles and battles to the host in order to communicate, interact and be accepted. Such translations of identities, cultures and battles brought from home can be conducted via different strategies – diasporas can foreignise or domesticate, or both. Such strategies can shift spatially, temporally and in relation to how well the host community is willing to listen. Both domestication and foreignisation strategies of diasporas and their consequences need unpacking by diaspora scholars. How do diasporas foreignise? Do they mistranslate? How do diasporas mediate the hierarchies in both cultures? Do they resist domestication, and how? Do they engage in partial translation, or perhaps in 'opaque translation' (Karamcheti, 1995)? Do they turn 'moments of "not understanding" into "spaces for learning"' (White, 1995: 338)? To what extent and when do they smooth over differences? What do they leave out and why?

A second important consequence of translation for diaspora research is that, through foreignisation strategies, diasporas have been, and continue to remain, a corrective to colonialism. If diaspora is conceptualised as an agent of decolonisation, the foreignising and domestication strategies of diasporas in achieving unlearning and decolonisation arise as legitimate research questions. Such a perspective can help us to move our focus away from an examination of the internal dynamics of a diasporic community and of their homeland – a useful yet dominant aspect of single-case study diasporic research today – to how diasporas have intervened in and shaped the culture and debates in the new home and globally. Hence, how diasporas dislodge coloniality today emerges as a central area of research. As bell hooks (1995: 298) argues, 'by transforming the oppressor's language, making a culture of resistance, Black people created an intimate speech that could say far more than was permissible within the boundaries of standard English'. In a similar vein, I propose that we shift our focus to an exploration of how diasporas have foreignised and pushed the boundaries of the Global North as well as how they continue to do so today. Chapter 3 expands further on this idea through a conceptualisation of diaspora as decolonisation.

Notes

1   It has been noted that in his 'The Task of the Translator', Benjamin's (1968) approach 'involves a curious mixture of Platonic views of meaning and more modern attitudes, of positivist and postpositivist elements' (Tymoczko, 2007: 48). While this has made it a paradise for drawing quotes, having something for everyone, it raises issues of epistemological coherence.
2   Dominated diaspora: a diasporic group not originating from a hegemonic culture, background or country (i.e. not a British expat).

3

Diaspora as decolonisation: 'Making a fuss' in diaspora and in the homeland

> My mother and my uncles are from that generation that would not make a fuss. Their attitude was that we were guests in this country and we should be grateful and not cause trouble, but I am not a guest here – I was born here. I don't know Jamaica where my mum is from, or Barbados where my father is from.
>
> (Benjamin Zephaniah, 2009)

As I began to discuss in the earlier chapters, another reason for introducing conceptualisations of translation is that through their translations and foreignisations, diasporas have the potential to become agents of decolonisation in both the homeland and the new home. Diasporas bring various disruptions and destabilisations to the Global North. I see the provincialising and decolonising carried out by postcolonial diasporas as a form of 'talking back' to the metropole. If empires used translation for creating and sustaining a system of coloniality and for governance, exploitation and conversion, can diasporic translations act as a challenge to colonisation through the previously conquered peoples talking back to the Global North, in the North? If translation was instrumental in defining the hierarchical construction of the core and the periphery, can diasporas, as the Global South in the Global North, be conceived as challenging those bifurcations and dislodging coloniality? Moreover, can the 'undoing' carried out by certain diasporas be extended to examine the interventions they make to the home, decolonising the homeland from a distance? Can it turn into an opportunity to see, reread and decolonise the home? For example, can the Kurdish diaspora be seen as intervening and interrupting the 'Turkishness contract' and 'de-Turkifying'

(Demir, 2014, 2017a; Unlu, 2016). I see these two types of possible interventions and undoings of diasporas, and conceive them under the theme of 'diaspora as decolonisation'. In this chapter, I focus on the dislodging of coloniality in the Global North.

Anthropology and colonisation produced and legitimised differentials of power between cultures and peoples. Anthropologists were instrumental in translating the periphery to the metropole, to their own audiences. Instead of extending their own analyst understandings and seeing the limits of their own language and world-views, Victorian anthropologists wrote about others in a way that restricted other cultures to the world-views of the metropole. As I will show below, they at times employed the prism of 'primitive versus civilised peoples'. They created analyst categories that failed to represent accurately the cultures and world-views they aimed to understand. By doing so, they not only created inconsistencies between their observer categories and the user categories and beliefs they sought to explain, but also eased and legitimised colonialism. Such problematic constructions and translations of 'alien' beliefs have been questioned by other anthropologists as well as by historians and sociologists. They should be understood as examples of what Holmwood and Stewart (1991) have called 'vertical fallacies'. However, such problematic constructions and fallacies are also questioned by postcolonial diasporas, through their political activism and intellectual engagement. In order to explore how diasporas decolonise, I will first discuss examples of vertical fallacies created by Victorian anthropology.

Accounting for others' beliefs: Vertical fallacy, anthropology and translation

Since it will be useful to my argument, I will go back to the discussions from the 1960s that revolved around the problems related to the practices of anthropologists. These discussions, some of which were compiled in Wilson (1970), tried to come to terms with the issue of how to account for 'alien' beliefs – that is, beliefs with which the inquirer is unfamiliar in their own culture. The contributors to this book discussed the problems that arise out of understanding a set of 'alien' beliefs, focusing mainly on how to interpret and describe an 'alien' thought system. There were many varying positions, but the issue essentially boiled down to whether or not there were alternative rationalities, specific to different cultures. My aim here is not to discuss rationality *per se*, but more specifically to dwell on the different options the contributors to this book, and anthropologists elsewhere (especially Lévy-Bruhl, Beattie and Evans-Pritchard), offered in relation to the problems arising out of the interpretation of 'alien' belief systems that are culturally remote from that of the inquirer. By so doing, I hope to explain vertical fallacy, and later discuss how postcolonial diasporas are part and parcel of overcoming it. It is therefore very useful to see what ideas the different sides of the anthropology debate put forward with respect to understanding other belief systems.

Various sides of the debate about how to account for 'alien' belief systems are presented and discussed in Wilson (1970), and in the related works of anthropologists. I will discuss the three main positions. I do not agree completely with any of these three positions, and will show the shortcomings of each below. However, what is important for this book is the shortcoming of the first two positions, namely the inconsistency that exists between the analyst categories and the user categories and beliefs. The criticism that can be developed for these two positions is central to understanding how vertical fallacies are created, and also to challenging them.

The first position, which might be called the 'Victorian approach', argues that the 'alien' belief systems are pre-logical (Lévy-Bruhl, 1985) or simply erroneous (Frazer, 1980). This position, very rarely defended today, has even argued that the mindset of the 'native' is intellectually confused, inferior or mistaken. How else could one account for the Nuer statement that human twins are birds? How else could one make sense of Australian Aboriginal people's assertion that the sun is a white cockatoo?

James Frazer (1980) argued that 'natives' believe in magic because they reason erroneously from their observations. On the other hand, Lucien Lévy-Bruhl (1985), who can be regarded as the Victorian *par excellence*, argued that 'primitive' thought differed from 'civilised' mentality both in quality and degree. He stated that 'primitive' people did not have the same conception of causality as the 'civilised', that they were indifferent to contradiction in a way the 'civilised' were not and that they reasoned differently because their reasoning was oriented towards the supernatural. A closer reading of Lévy-Bruhl's works shows that he did not deserve some of the harsh criticisms he received thereafter.[1] However, I think it is worth discussing them here, especially in relation to the point I wish to raise about user and observer categories.

Lévy-Bruhl (1985) argued that objective causal explanation was specific to 'civilised' cultures and mystical explanations were specific to 'primitive' cultures, which he called 'pre-logical'. He then went on to argue that this specific reasoning and the mystical explanations that went hand in hand made it possible for the 'natives', for example, to believe that a man was killed by a buffalo because he was bewitched. The 'civilised', on the other hand would not hold such beliefs because their explanations were causal, not supernatural. By way of constructing two observer categories, namely making a distinction between the 'civilised' and 'primitive' mentality and attributing the latter to the 'alien' cultures, I argue that Lévy-Bruhl not only misrepresented the reasoning by 'natives', but also read contradiction into their activity – albeit a contradiction that he could not recognise. A quotation from Evans-Pritchard makes this clear:

> Lévy-Bruhl is also wrong in supposing that there is necessarily a contradiction between an objective causal explanation and a mystical one. It is not so. The two kinds of explanation can be, as indeed they are, held together, the one supplementing the other; and they are therefore not exclusive. For example, the dogma that death is due to witchcraft does not exclude the observation that the man was killed by a buffalo. For Lévy-Bruhl there is here a contradiction, to which natives are indifferent. But no contradiction is involved. On the contrary, the natives are making a very acute analysis of the situation. They are perfectly aware that a buffalo killed the man, but they hold that he would not have been killed by it if he had not been bewitched. Why otherwise should he have been killed by it, why he and not someone else, why by that buffalo and not by another, why at that time and place and not at another?
>
> (Evans-Pritchard, 1981: 129, 130)

Here, then, we see an inconsistency between Lévy-Bruhl's categorisations and the categorisations of the 'natives'. Of course, I am not arguing that 'alien' belief systems are totally consistent or immune from inconsistencies. I am only saying that Lévy-Bruhl's attribution of 'a lack of a causal explanation' to them is a misrepresentation of the 'alien' belief system. This is because Lévy-Bruhl's categorisations divorce the two types of reasoning – the causal and the mystical – and attribute the latter to the 'natives', whereas the 'natives' use both the causal and the mystical in their reasoning. Thus Lévy-Bruhl's categorisations are in contradiction with the user categories. Just like other groups, 'natives' not only reason mystically but also causally, and this should have been reflected in Lévy-Bruhl's account of them. Lévy-Bruhl's categorisations therefore should be jettisoned (or reconstructed) because, as they are, they misrepresent the belief system of the 'natives'.[2]

A second problem with this Victorian approach – especially as presented by its proponents Tylor and Frazer – is that of seeing the 'alien' belief system in terms of the concepts and categories that the inquirer borrows from their own culture. In other words, the Victorians tried to make the 'alien' beliefs intelligible to their own society by using the meanings they carry over from their own culture. This leads to a misidentification of the concepts and categorisations used by the 'alien' culture. Obviously there is nothing wrong *per se* in seeing and pointing to similar concepts and categorisations that may exist in the inquirer's culture and that of the 'alien' – or, for that matter, creating or using observer concepts with which the 'native' may not be familiar but that are consistent with user behaviour. But trying to understand the 'alien' thought system just by resorting to the categories and concepts that exist in the inquirer's culture without any concern for user categories and concepts is a recipe for poor interpretations.

This other approach to the interpretation of 'alien' cultures, which is usually referred to as the Symbolist approach, is influenced by Durkheimian sociology (e.g. Beattie, 1964; Leach, 1954). The Symbolist does not attribute intellectual deficiency or error to the adherents of the 'alien' belief system, but instead argues that 'alien' belief systems should not be taken at face value. The Symbolist approach argues that 'alien' thought systems should be accounted for by taking the beliefs of the 'natives' as metaphorical symbols and not as literal utterances.

Beattie, one of the proponents of this approach, does not agree with the Victorian approach's attribution of error to the 'alien' belief system or the description of it as 'prelogical'. He wants to go beyond the Victorian approach and argues:

> It was easy for the Victorians to assume that such thinking as they did was simple and 'childish' (this was one of their favourite adjectives); a very inferior version of their own. The intensive fieldwork which was to provide an intimate understanding of 'simpler' people's way of life and thought, and so to demonstrate the superficiality and inadequacy of such views, had not begun.
>
> (Beattie, 1964: 65)

In order to go beyond the Victorian approach, Beattie makes a distinction between scientific cultures and non-scientific cultures, and argues that in non-scientific cultures, the world has a symbolic character. For Beattie, beliefs in magical powers, witches, sorcerers, spirits and so on actually represent symbols of 'more or less abstract notions like power, group solidarity, familial or political authority' (Beattie, 1964: 70). His analysis of magic and ritual in 'alien' societies thus rests on an understanding that regards such activities as mainly expressive and symbolic. He states:

> It is a function of ritual to enhance the social importance of something which is held to be of value in the society which has the ritual. If ritual is a kind of language, a way of saying things, then Trobriand canoe magic stresses the importance of canoe building for the Trobrianders; blood pact ritual emphasizes the need for mutual support between parties to it; the avoidance ritual asserts the need to maintain good relations between affinally linked groups.
>
> (Beattie, 1964: 210)

In this way, Beattie hopes we can explain the 'alien' belief system without calling it pre-logical or erroneous, or describing it in any other way that may attribute intellectual deficiency to the adherents of that belief system. Symbolic interpretation, Beattie argues, does not commit the sin of 'attempting arbitrarily to impose our own category distinctions on those of other cultures' (Beattie, 1964: 212). Understanding magic, ritual, sorcery and so on in a symbolic way, he argues, overcomes the Victorian approach's shortcomings.[3]

At the core of this approach, then, is the burden on the anthropologist's shoulders to transcend the framework of the 'natives' themselves. In fact, transcending the notions of the actors (the 'natives') is seen as essential in order to uncover the 'alien' belief system. The 'native' may not be prepared to acknowledge that his beliefs and corresponding utterances are symbolic and expressive, but the Symbolist insists that they are understood as such. Beattie argues:

> The total procedures which we label 'magical' need not be, and often are not, viewed by their practitioners as purely symbolic (or even as symbolic at all). They are ways of getting what they want, what is done in such and such a situation in a given culture.
>
> (Beattie, 1970: 251)

But Beattie continues to argue that 'nevertheless they involve … a symbolic element' (Beattie, 1970: 251, 252).

Here, then, we see that Beattie imposes symbolic meaning to the whole 'alien' culture, at least some aspects of which may not necessarily have a symbolic element in that culture. Such imputations of meaning that are not consistent with the 'alien' thought system will necessarily create inconsistencies between the observer categories and concepts, and user behaviours. Thus, while Lévy-Bruhl imposed category distinctions that were not consistent with the 'alien' culture, Beattie imputes symbolic meaning to the 'alien' belief system, which in a similar way is a misrepresentation of that thought system. This difficulty with the Symbolist model is discussed by Papineau:

> According to the symbolist, when a native explains his devotions at some shrine by saying that he is showing respect to the spirits of his ancestors, whose shrine it is, we should not take his assertion at face value, but rather understand him as referring to his kinship group and expressing its importance to his social being. His actions, correspondingly, should be read as not *really* aimed instrumentally at appeasing any spirits, but rather as a *symbolic* performance enacting the social significance of his kinship group.
>
> (Papineau, 1978: 145)

Obviously, some of the expressions of the 'natives' may be metaphorical, but the Symbolist's mistake is to interpret the expressions in the 'alien' culture, or at least those they cannot understand, as *tout court* metaphorical.[4] Just as metaphors exist in English, they can exist in other languages and cultures. The solution for which I argue does not deny the existence of metaphors in 'alien' cultures, but rather demands that when the anthropologist argues that the 'native' is speaking in a metaphorical way, this must really be the case. To do this, one must refrain from the Symbolist's insistence that the *whole* 'alien' culture is a figurative version of something else. In other words, observer categories should not do violence to the others' culture in their translations and recognise that mistranslations have created racialised hierarchies and justified the domination and exploitations of others.

Challenging vertical fallacies

I introduced the earlier discussion of epistemology and anthropology[5] for three reasons. First, translators and anthropologists encounter similar problems (Gentzler, 2001: 178). How do you interpret other cultures? How do you write about another culture in another language? How do you ensure you do not misrepresent another culture and what is said? 'Translation is one of the things that ethnographers undertake (together with analysis and description) in order to give readers an understanding of the beliefs and practices of unfamiliar peoples' (Asad, 1995: 226). A second, related reason is that such epistemic vertical fallacies have worked in parallel with colonial power hierarchies. They have reinforced, reproduced and justified colonial domination and exploitation of vast parts of the world. Even today, their legacy continues as they legitimise the subjugation, poverty and backwardness of the Global South. We thus need to not only recognise the close relationship between epistemological fallacies and power relationships, but also that their undoing needs a simultaneous intervention. Third, the discussion above shows how anthropology and translation were central to the way the Global South was constructed by the Global North. Diasporas have questioned such constructions. They have spoken back, and challenged North-centric world-views. I argue that diasporas should not simply be seen as mediators, but rather as agents who speak back and challenge the world-views in the Global North, aiding foreignisation and decolonisation of the new home. They also speak back and challenge world-views in the home left behind, aiding decolonisation of the homeland at a distance.

Diaspora as Global South in the Global North: Undoing colonisation

Radical remembering

If diaspora is a leftover of colonialism, empire and nation-building, then considering its potential for decolonisation is necessary.[6] Postcolonial diasporas, together with solidarity from other groups, have been central to the building of resistance against the airbrushing of colonialism, slavery and exploitation and its relationship to today. Diasporas have also played a central role in interrupting silences and speaking about empires, slavery and injustice. That they work to invert the vertical fallacy that the Victorian anthropologists created and refuse to be fitted into a world-view defined by the Global North is significant. Yet the role of postcolonial diasporas in challenging the world-views in the Global North has rarely been a central aspect of theorisations of diaspora. Even when it has been taken up and applied, it has not been an important aspect of conceptualisations of diaspora but has often helped us to develop more nuanced understandings of race and ethnicity (e.g. the works of Hall and Gilroy).

The intervention of diasporas in global political reordering and on decolonisation is not a recent phenomenon. Intellectual resistance and activism of the African diaspora in the West stretches back to the eighteenth and nineteenth centuries (Mosley, 2017). Ignatius Sancho, Olaudah Equiano and Quobna Cugoano were the leaders of 'Sons of Africa', a group of emancipated slaves in eighteenth-century London. They exposed the horrors of the slave trade, campaigned and wrote letters to MPs and newspapers and joined forces with abolitionist movements. In the United States, David Walker, Martin Delaney, Frederick Douglass, Alexander Crummell and Edward Blyden in the nineteenth century developed scholarship and made interventions, especially challenging scientific and intellectual accounts that legitimised slavery and oppression. The activism and scholarship of the African diaspora in Western metropoles in the eighteenth and nineteenth centuries were central not only in opposing slavery and domination, but also made central contributions to the development of the notions of freedom and liberty in the West. Douglass, for example, championed women's rights along with the plight of the African Americans. Around the same time John Stuart Mill's (1869) *The Subjection of Women* came out, Douglass was also writing about and advocating the women's cause and drawing solidarities between oppressions. He spoke in favour of women's rights and suffrage at the International Council of Women in Washington, DC, and published in 1871 in *The Woman's Journal* (Douglass, 1999 [1871]). He rejected racialised notions of freedom, justice and equality, showing the limits of the then-existing conceptualisations of freedom. Besides championing the rights of African Americans, he made intellectual contributions, expanding freedom and emancipation for others:

> We ask that as injustice knows no rich, no poor, no black, no white, but, like the government of God, renders alike to every man reward or punishment, according as his works shall be – the white and black man may stand upon an equal footing before the laws of the land.
>
> (Douglass, 1999 [1871]: 262)

If we look at recent history, there are many examples of radical remembering and reordering led by diasporas, and through initiatives driven by activists and institutions in conversation and solidarity with diasporas. The UK reparations movement's Birmingham Declaration (Africa Reparations Movement (UK) 1994), the Black Cultural Archives initiative and the campaigning by the children of the Amritsar massacre for recognition (Bilkhu, 2019) are three relatively recent examples of radical remembering. These build on the resistance and campaigning of their first-generation parents and grandparents (Sivanandan, 1982). Postcolonial diasporas have also challenged the teaching of history in schools and in museums. For example, there is now an International Slavery Museum in Liverpool, the focus of which is slavery itself (rather than keeping the focus on the more easily digestible British abolition story). The museum does not just examine the horrors of the slave trade, but also underlines that the city, and Britain, obtained much wealth from the trade. From Black Lives Matter to #Rhodes Must Fall to Virtual Migrants' various art and media projects that explore race, global justice and art, to the Royal Geography Society's Bristol Walk, which divulges the dark secrets of half a million Africans who were brought to Bristol, to the revealing and shaming of the newspaper advertisement of the Leicester City Council, which tried to discourage Ugandan Asians from coming to Leicester in 1972 (BBC, 2012), an increasing number of initiatives and activism of

diasporas now exist, which lay bare unsavoury truths, and interrupt the silences and the whitewashed accounts of history in the
United Kingdom. Such truths are being taken to 'White spaces',
to the British countryside. That many UK National Trust country
houses have connections, if not owe their existence, to the empire,
to the Caribbean and East India Company has long been an inconvenient truth – not seen as worthy of interrupting a lovely Sunday
visit to a National Trust property with such 'unpleasantries'. But
they are now being explored by the Colonial Countryside Project
(Project, 2021; Fowler, 2020). It was, of course, not just the landed
gentry and the new middle classes in England and Scotland who
financed and profited from the empire and the slave trade – part
of the wealth trickled down to the rest of the population in the
British Isles, to the financing and establishing of the welfare state,
and some of it also went to finance White settler colonies – for
example, New Zealand and Australia.

The African American diaspora and its struggles, the civil rights
movement and the activism of Martin Luther King and the Black
Panthers were of course central to decolonisation of the metropole.
We should see Black Lives Matter, Black History Month, and 'reverse
pedagogy in the metropole' (Gopal, 2019) as part and parcel of
this radical remembering. However, it should be acknowledged that
these critical interruptions have also awakened a resistance to racial
remembering. There is a backlash to remembering and bringing
to the fore the previously omitted and whitewashed stories, and
knowledges and injustices – whether by columnists condemning the
National Trust for revealing connections between its properties and
the slave trade and empire as it goes against the story of the nation
they wish to project (e.g. Moore, 2020), or those booing players
in football matches for taking the knee as a sign of respect and
demand for racial justice. Postcolonial diasporas have also sought
what I have called radical remembering in other parts of the Global
North – for example, in France. Two organisations, namely Conseil
Répresentatif des Associations Noires (CRAN), an umbrella organisation of Black activists, and the Indigènes de la République in
France, are two examples of campaigning led by diasporas. They
question colonialism and other unpalatable aspects of history. Like
many other postcolonial diasporas, activists of these organisations
should not be understood as 'memorial activists' focused on the

past. In fact, they are attempting to deploy 'the past in order to talk about the present', drawing attention to reparations and to the racism faced by postcolonial diasporas in France (Lotem, 2016: 293–4). All in all, diasporas have been central to the decentring of the metropole, challenging strategic ignorance (Bailey, 2007). They have sought to contest the ways in which the national history has typically been told and to attempt to reshape what constitutes French, British, American or other Global Northern history and icons. Such decentrings of diasporas are, of course, part and parcel of overall decolonisation demands – and their aim has been to shift understandings of yesterday in order to develop better and more accurate understandings of today.

Yet there is much resistance to radical remembering. It is useful to think about it *vis-à-vis* the phrase 'Lest we forget'. This is a well-known phrase seen at war memorial sites throughout the United Kingdom, New Zealand and Australia. It insists on remembering those who made sacrifices, who fought and died in war and conflict. It is the iconic motto of Remembrance Day, and it is closely associated with World War I. Even though Remembrance Day and this phrase have been expanded to cover 'other' wars and conflicts, it is not used for remembering conflict and violence associated with slavery, colonialism or the violence of empires.[7] When it comes to these, the limits of memory and compassion become obvious. They can instead be neatly sealed, refusing to be extended. Diasporas are asked to 'get over it'. Remembering and forgetting are also topics of contention in the United States, whereby activists talk about the repeated mantra of 'Never forget 9/11' being uttered by the very same people who usually tell African Americans to 'get over' slavery. Similarly in Turkey, the Gallipoli victory is remembered at the highest level while the violent suffering of Armenians is denied (Gocek, 2014). The remembering is, yet again, carried on by the diaspora.

Remembering those who made sacrifices and died in war and conflict is rightly called for. However, diasporas have also highlighted what is remembered and what is conveniently forgotten and erased, especially by juxtaposing remembering against the amnesia of empire (Khan, 2015, 2017; Singh, 2017).[8] We are still far from being in a position where the raising of such issues does not guarantee trivialisations such as '"It" did not really happen; it was not that bad, or that important' (Trouillot, 1995: 96). Narratives that 'sweeten the horror or banalize' via utterances such as 'some [African American slaves] were better fed than British workers' (Trouillot, 1995: 97) are still heard. But abject denial, or at least strategic ignorance, is increasingly being challenged. The presence and activism of diasporas in the Global North have been central to this. Our understandings of diaspora should not just recognise, but make pivotal, the role of diasporas in reshaping and reordering the global political orders through their radical remembering, resistance and decolonising.

Radical inclusion

The decolonisation role of diasporas does not need to be reduced to them speaking about the evils of empire and colonisation. It is also there in terms of changing the national story and demanding radical inclusion in the new home. If we think about how postcolonial diasporas can shift the national story in the 'new' place, we have to go back to diasporic activists – for example, Ambalavaner Sivanandan, who drew attention to the fact that colonial history is deeply intertwined with the presence of diasporas in the Global North, exemplified in the memorable motto 'we are here because you were there'. It tied up postwar 'migration' from Africa, Asia and the Caribbean with the empire, and with today's metropole. 'We are here because you were there' is critical: it makes an intervention in both spatial and temporal terms. It connects today with the past, and the current postwar diasporas with the 'White' population. Even if such reminders are not always listened to, the diasporas can, at times, challenge the metropole through reminders, as they did in the Windrush Scandal of 2018. In relation to it, David Lammy (2019), MP for Tottenham, said:

> The Windrush story does not begin in 1948; the Windrush story begins in the 17th century, when British slave traders stole 12 million Africans from their homes, took them to the Caribbean and sold them into slavery to work on plantations. The wealth of this country was built on the backs of the ancestors of the Windrush generation. We are here today because you were there.
>
> My ancestors were British subjects, but they were not British subjects because they came to Britain. They were British subjects

because Britain came to them, took them across the Atlantic, colonised them, sold them into slavery, profited from their labour and made them British subjects. That is why I am here, and it is why the Windrush generation are here.

There is no British history without the history of the empire. As the late, great Stuart Hall put it: 'I am the sugar at the bottom of the English cup of tea.'

The Windrush children are imprisoned in this country – as we have seen of those who have been detained – centuries after their ancestors were shackled and taken across the ocean in slave ships. They are pensioners imprisoned in their own country. That is a disgrace, and it happened here because of a refusal to remember our history.

Postcolonial diasporas have been, and continue to present themselves as being, constitutive of the national/metropole story, and in so doing they have resisted the segregated way in which White European history and stories of postwar 'immigration' are told. In their chapter entitled 'White past, multicultural present: heritage and national stories', Naidoo and Littler (2004: 334) question the tired old divide that is created and recreated between the White past and multicultural present, and more particularly the ways in which Britain reinforced 'non-white presence as foreign' in schools and other institutions, such as in the heritage sector. In the heritage and culture sector, 'their' culture was 'translated into something that white people could taste or watch or enjoy without having to think critically about their own racist behaviour or how institutions reinforced racist practices' and promoted 'the myth of British culture as white and hermetically sealed before the advent of postwar migration' (Naidoo and Littler, 2004: 335). There is now academic work showing how modernity and nations were created through waves of migration questioning the telling of postwar migration as a celebratory phenomenon (e.g. Alexander, 2000; Bhambra, 2007; Fryer, 1984; Meer, 2015; Pearce et al., 2013; Shilliam, 2015, 2018; Virdee, 2014; Visram, 1986; Wemyss, 2009). However, this desire for what I call radical inclusion is also articulated through activists and a new generation of diasporic writers and campaigners, such as Akala (2018), Eddo-Lodge (2018), Hirsh (2018), Pitts (2020) and Shukla (2017).

Another aspect of this decolonisation is, of course, about how the enslaved and colonial subjects were not merely victims of this nation's [Britain] imperial history and subsequent beneficiaries of its crises of conscience, but rather, agents whose resistance not only contributed to their own freedom but also put pressure on and reshaped British ideas about freedom.

(Gopal, 2016: 24)

Through tracing rebellions and resistance in the colonies – for example, the Urabi Revolt, the Haitian revolution, the Sepoy Mutiny and the Morant Bay Uprising – Gopal (2016, 2019) argues that such rebellions and resistance were fundamental to how freedom was understood in the colonies, and through them in the imperial centre. Naidoo and Littler (2004: 335) also make us rethink this through heritage: how Asian women in *shalwaar-kameze* need to be understood not just as a tokenistic part of today's multi-racial Britain, presented on inclusive leaflets, but as being part of the British workers' rights movement, as activists who played a significant role through their resistance against the empire. They led, among others, the Bristol Bus Boycott (1963), the Imperial Typewriters Strike (1974), the Grunwick Dispute (1976), the activism following the New Cross Fire (1981) and resistance against Gate Gourmet in 2005. They challenged understandings of freedom and equality and dignity, expanding human rights. Such examples help us think through radical ways in which diasporas need to be included into the national history and present, rather than rehearse the often-repeated vertical fallacies that reproduce hierarchical worldviews: 'civilised enlightened West' versus 'unruly elsewhere'; 'freedom loving Europe' versus 'authoritarian else-where'; or 'our White yesterday' versus 'our racially diverse today'. Such fallacies not only do injustice to others by erasing them and making diasporic peoples have to justify their existence in the Global North; they also do injustice to the Global North as they stand in the way of understanding the self and one's own history beyond self-congratulatory national narratives.

Radical remembering and inclusion versus the rhetoric of 'social inclusion'

What do we see when we compare such demands of diasporas for what I call radical remembering and radical inclusion with the 'social inclusion rhetoric'? In this section, I will discuss this social inclusion rhetoric with regard to two diasporic communities in the United Kingdom: the South Asian and Afro-Caribbean communities. The social inclusion rhetoric became pervasive during the New Labour years, especially following the Cantle Report (Cantle, 2001), commissioned by New Labour's Home Secretary David Blunkett and written by Ted Cantle in response to the riots in Bradford, Oldham and Burnley. This social inclusion rhetoric dominated the ensuing decades and continues to shape the United Kingdom's engagement with its diasporas. On the whole, the rhetoric of 'social inclusion' assumes a problem of lack of assimilation and lack of citizenship on the part of the newcomers. It peddles the view that 'postcolonial diasporas' do not share our values, but rather segregate and create parallel lives. Since the 2001 Oldham riots, which saw clashes between South Asian youth and White youth, this social inclusion agenda has come to shape firmly dominant forms of understanding of certain groups, especially South Asians and Muslims in the United Kingdom.

The problem is typically constructed as 'too much culture' on the part of South Asians, and the offered solution is to socially include them – for example, through the teaching of British values in schools, calling on them to speak English and the introduction of the UK citizenship test. The presentation of what constitutes 'a social problem' is, of course, an expression of power. The identification of such problems is usually accompanied by, if not used as a justification for, the solution/policy that was envisaged in the first place. Asians who, in the previous decades, were positively 'portrayed in the [British] media as being hard-working, as having strong families and cultures' (Kushnick, 1993: 18) had over time become a threat. Now they were seen as having 'too much culture'. This culture was getting in the way of social inclusion. As Miah, Sanderson and Thomas (2020: 10) discuss, such discourses about the culture and religion of others are not new, and were employed against East European Jewish migrants and Irish Catholics who arrived in England in the nineteenth century; they were seen as 'dark strangers with an alien and threatening culture and religion'. Young, who examined the 2001 Oldham riots, presented one of the earliest criticisms of this social inclusion rhetoric. He argued that urban disturbances and riots do not occur due to lack of assimilation into the dominant value system, in this case Britishness. He argued that riots occur where the diasporas are absorbed culturally but excluded socially. Cultural inclusion of diasporas, as we know, occurs through mass education, media, national curriculum, youth culture and so on, and social exclusion through economic deprivation, prejudice, racism and becoming aware of lack of opportunities. Unlike their first-generation parents who 'knew their place', newer generations are not scared to show their discontent and disagreement:

> disturbance occurs because of the degree of assimilation, it is a function of becoming more 'like us' [i.e. British] rather than being unlike us. It is assimilation or integration that allows structural exclusion and lack of opportunities of work ... to be experienced as unfair. Asian youths who rioted in the northern towns had the same accents and expectations as the white youths who rioted on the other side of the ethnic line. They scarcely needed teaching citizenship or English ...
>
> (Young, 2003: 458)

The recommendations of the 2001 Cantle Report and the subsequent introduction of the citizenship test, of the teaching of British values and so on of course become all too absurd in the context of rioters being born, bred and schooled in the United Kingdom, never mind the report's poor understanding of the problems associated with the 2001 riots – especially the anger and frustration associated with issues of inequality, resentment and racism (Bagguley and Hussain, 2012). It instead largely lays the problem with South Asians, their culture and their failure to integrate without questioning – for example, racialised housing policies, White flight from schools or the reduction in support systems from the state. It demands critical scrutiny of cultural others and excludes them from the narrative of the nation while accusing them of failing to integrate.

Such social inclusion rhetoric strategies and policies should therefore make us rethink exactly to whom this discourse is directed. Who is the audience to which it is geared? I suggest that social inclusion is a rhetoric aimed at the 'natives' – they reassure the 'natives' that something is being done to protect the (White) British and Britishness through underlining that something is being done about others' 'cultural excess' – that it is being curbed. Similar discourses of 'inclusion' have also been questioned with regard to other initiatives for 'inclusion', such as the UK citizenship test, one of its offspring. Again, the inclusive merit here is deemed to be minimal. Bartram (2019), for example, argues that citizenship requirements in fact harm integration rather than boosting it, thus reinforcing Fortier's (2017) research that the citizenship test is there to relieve the worries and anxieties of the 'native population'.

While the South Asian diaspora were problematised as having 'too much culture', Afro-Caribbean diasporas have had to put up with the accusations of a 'lack of culture'. Afro-Caribbeans have typically been portrayed as 'lacking the characteristics of hard work, ambition, commitment to education, and strong families and cultures' (Kushnick, 1993: 18). Benson's (1996) title 'Asians Have Culture, West Indians Have Problems' aptly summarises this (Alexander, 2018). The problems faced by the Afro-Caribbean and African American diasporas have been attributed to 'their lack of appropriate social inclusion and socialisation'. Such racialised perspectives are associated with what are known as 'deficit theories'. They are linked to Charles Murray's (1990, 1996) notion of 'underclass', which he applied to both the United States and the United Kingdom. For Murray (2019), the underclass is not just the poor; it is those people 'cut off from mainstream American life'. In his view, the welfare state enables this by supporting the poor. His form of inclusion of the underclass envisioned that welfare support be withdrawn. According to his argument, this cut in 'welfare dependency'[9] would push the underclass to join the dominant culture – in other words, it would 'include' through exclusion and hardship.

As discussed above, the rhetoric of underclass, deficit theories and 'lack of culture' are often called upon in the media and wider public discourse in relation to the African and Black diaspora (Shilliam, 2018). A lack of social inclusion in this case is associated with not having the 'correct' (British/American, etc.) values. It was easily resorted to during the 2011 London riots. It overlooked frustrations associated with inequality, akin to the 2001 Oldham riots.[10] Instead of dealing with the consequences of poverty (poor skills, poor housing, low income, unemployment, family breakdown, gangs) the media and public discussions on the 2011 London riots, like the 2001 Oldham riots, sought to focus on values – or rather the lack of appropriate values on the part of the rioters and their families. The then Work and Pensions Secretary, Iain Duncan Smith, whose ideas on family, inclusion and poverty are close to those of Charles Murray (Slater, 2012: 949) argued that the 2011 riots were underpinned by a gang culture. Then Prime Minister David Cameron also argued that 'gangs were at the heart of the protests and have been behind the coordinated attacks' (Khan, 2018). The ordinary respectable 'natives' were reassured that rioters and gangs would be punished when in fact 'evidence of the influence of gangs proved hard to find and official analyses of the riots and their aftermath, including those by the police service had little to say about the role of gangs in either the violence or looting' (Metropolitan Police Service, 2012; Newburn et al., 2015: 997). Others reproduced this deficit theory on the BBC's *Newsnight* (BBC, 2011).

All in all, we can see that about a decade after the Oldham riots, the social inclusion rhetoric was deployed, again by pointing to a group for not having the right values. It was deployed for another diaspora with a twist. While the 2001 Oldham riots highlighted 'too much culture' on the part of South Asians, the 2011 London riots focused on a 'lack of culture' on the part of the Black diaspora.

Such deficit theories have, of course, long been challenged. For example, Nightingale (1993) and Bourgois (2003) have challenged the view that there is a lack of socialisation on the part of the Black 'underclass'. Their work show that the group deemed to be the underclass embodies the values of the dominant culture in the United States. With respect to the Puerto Rican diaspora in East Harlem, following a five-year ethnographic fieldwork project, Bourgois (2003: 326) argues:

> They are not 'exotic others' operating in an irrational netherworld. On the contrary they are 'made in America'. Highly motivated, ambitious inner-city youths who have been attracted to the multi-million dollar drug economy ... precisely because they believe in ... the American dream.
>
> Like most other people in the US [they] are scrambling to obtain their piece of the pie as fast as possible. In fact, in their pursuit of

success they are even following the minute details of the classical yankee model for upward mobility. They are aggressively pursuing careers as private entrepreneurs; they take risks, work hard, and pray for good luck. They are the ultimate rugged individualists braving an unpredictable frontier where fortune, fame, and destruction are just around the corner ...

Nightingale's (1993) study of poor African Americans in Philadelphia also questioned them being anything other than truly American, embodying American culture and values, questioning the detached Black underclass model. An equivalent of this argument was also peddled during the 2011 London riots. Questioning such deficit models, Nightingale's ethnographic study argued that 'it was only by getting to know some poor urban African-American children much closer up that I could grasp just how thoroughly American their lives have been' (Nightingale, 1993: 5).

In summary, the social inclusion rhetoric and responses employed in relation to the South Asian and Afro-Caribbean diasporas in the United Kingdom are in fact part and parcel of the significant exclusion and othering faced by diasporas. Since the early 2000s, 'issues of religion, ethnicity and identity moved centre-stage, with evocations of "parallel lives" and "community cohesion" conjuring familiar and well-worn tropes of cultural difference and incompatibility that resonated strongly with the earlier "race relations" framework' (Alexander, 2018: 1043). The othering of diasporas in the current period in the United Kingdom can be identified through the introduction of the Prevent Agenda, the Trojan Horse Scandal (Holmwood and O'Toole, 2017; Miah, 2017), the Windrush Scandal, Go Home Vans (Jones et al., 2017), the problematisation of minority women and the pitting of 'their' culture against feminism (Bassel and Emejulu, 2018), the revoking of British citizenship of dual nationals (Prabhat, 2019), the presentation of multiculturalism and free speech being in crisis (Lentin and Titley, 2011; Titley, 2020), the abandonment of refugees by the state (Mayblin and James, 2019), the material and symbolic dimensions of border controls (Monforte, 2016) and so on. The language of social inclusion conceives of a largely untouched and sealed national story and identity to which diasporas are expected to bow to rather than conceiving of a national identity where a shared national story and identity are created and co-owned.

National identity has already changed, and continues to change, through the demands of, for example, the working class and women's movements. They have demanded radical inclusion and have resisted being erased from the national story and global accounts. Their history and contributions have become, or are on the fast track to becoming, comfortably part and parcel of British (or French, Italian, etc.) identity and history, as a simple glance at school history books will show. Enabled by the expansion and greater equalisation of universities, through the struggles of women and working-class people coming to positions of power, the Levellers, Suffragettes and Chartists are now part of British history and the national identity. Celebratory history continues, but these previously omitted histories are now part of many of the national stories of the Global North. I argue that national identity and global politics are also changing through the decolonisation and foreignisation that diasporas have brought and continue to bring, and through their activism and efforts for radical inclusion and remembering in local, national and global stories. Inequalities and discrimination were exposed by the Bristol Bus Boycott (1963), the Imperial Typewriters Strike (1974), the Grunwick Dispute (1976), the New Cross Fire (1981), the Windrush Scandal (2018), the Black Lives Matter movement and many others, such as the anti-Black Pete movement in the Netherlands and the Indigènes de la République in France. Accounts of such resistance will also need to be told as diasporas expand understandings of freedom, equality and dignity in the North and globally.

The issue, then, is whether or not academic scholarship will expand its existing categories and explanatory mechanisms, and shift our understanding of diaspora from mere stories of hybridity, migrancy, superdiversity and cosmopolitan sociability to accounts that make the role of diasporas central in foreignising and decolonising the Global North. The latter can include stories of hybridity and diversity, but they say much more. This book is an attempt to push the boundaries of diaspora scholarship, which has often been hemmed into debates on hybridity, or gardening tropes, or ideal type definitions. In the last two chapters, I have located the central tenets of diaspora as translation and as decolonisation. I argued that diasporas should be given the attention and primacy they deserve in decolonising the 'national' story, acting as the Global South in the Global North. Diaspora, of course, is not just the movement of peoples. What turns 'overseas' people who migrate into a diaspora, I argue, is that they speak back to the metropole; they bring ethics and politics together, they become the Global South in the Global North, intervening in decolonisation in the new home and/or in the home left behind. This requires the recognition of diasporas as agents of globalisation and of decolonisation rather than a pure outcome or consequence of these. Making translation and decolonisation central to our understanding of diaspora can therefore help us to not only rethink diaspora, but also place it at the centre of our understanding of modernity, globalisation and politics today.

Notes

1 Edward Evans-Pritchard (1981) argued that Lévy-Bruhl was criticised unduly harshly. He suggested that some of the undeserved criticisms arose from a misunderstanding of what Lévy-Bruhl was saying. See also Cazeneuve (1972) for a more subtle interpretation and defence of Lévy-Bruhl. Both Evans-Pritchard and Cazeneuve argue that Lévy-Bruhl did not see 'natives' as irrational or unintelligent but merely wanted to underline that they reasoned in a different way to people from 'civilised' cultures. In this respect, Lévy-Bruhl's views seem akin to those of Peter Winch (1964), who also argues that there are different criteria for reasoning, specific to each culture. Yet by using 'civilised' and 'native' reasoning, he inevitably introduced a racialised hierarchy rather than recognising difference.

2 It is worth emphasising that I am not arguing that concepts which the 'natives' do not use should not be used by the inquirer. I am only arguing that observer categories must be consistent with user actions.

3 Edward Evans-Pritchard (1971) also argues a similar version of this about the Nuer in his chapter about symbols.

4 My critique of the Symbolist here draws on David Papineau's (1978) useful chapter, 'Alien Belief Systems'.

5 Travel literature is, of course, similar to anthropology – both have reproduced imperialist discourses as they have created visions of other cultures for their own home/metropole consumption.

6 It goes without saying that not all migrant groups rise to this challenge. As I discussed in previous chapters, some can be ethno-parochial and chauvinistic too.

7 World War I was itself a European imperial war, of course.

8 In the United Kingdom, we have had statues for remembering animals who suffered in violence and conflict, yet there is no national memorial in the United Kingdom that commemorates the victims of Trans-Atlantic slavery. A World War I memorial for the 130,000 Sikh soldiers who fought for Britain was erected in 2015, but only after fundraising by the Sikhs in the United Kingdom. There are plans to have a national site in London.

9 Murray was invited by the Sunday Times to visit the United Kingdom. See Murray (1996), where Murray meets his critics and relates his theories to the United Kingdom.

10 The Ministry of Justice and Home Office background analysis highlighted that rioters came from the most deprived areas; more than 42 per cent of those arrested received free school meals; more than two-thirds had special educational needs (Ministry of Justice, 2012).

4

Translations and decolonisations of the Kurdish diaspora

I became a Kurd in London; I became a Kurd thanks to imperialists.
(Interview with Kurdish male, 58)

Foreignising translation and decolonisation are central ways in which diasporas speak back to and challenge the Global North. Anthropology and translation were instrumental in the establishment of the hierarchical construction of the core and periphery. In the last two chapters, I defended the argument that our conceptualisations of diaspora should make central the ways in which diasporas have been, and continue to remain, a corrective to colonialism. I also provided some examples of the decolonisation demands of South Asian and Afro-Caribbean diasporas in the United Kingdom for radical inclusion and radical remembering. Diasporas, however, not only dislodge coloniality in the new home, but as the Global South they also speak back to and aid the decolonisation of the home that has been left behind. In this chapter, I will examine the translational activities, interventions and undoings of the Kurdish diaspora in Europe. My aim is not only to show heuristically how some of the conceptualisations from previous chapters can be applied, but also how they can be extended further. Some of the analytical points that are developed and discussed – for example, 'transnational indigeneity' – are relevant and 'portable' (Polit and Beck, 2010) to other settings and diasporas, where the translation of ethno-political identity in diaspora is central. In fact, the Kurdish diaspora provides a good illustration of how a strong desire to translate ethno-political identity in diaspora maps onto indigeneity and decoloniality.

Many of the works on the Kurdish diaspora have carefully examined Kurds' antagonistic relationship with their countries of origin, be it Iran, Iraq, Syria or Turkey, or their political activities in diaspora in this respect. Kurds' mobilisation activities have been unpacked and discussed in detail (e.g. Akbarzadeh et al., 2020; Alinia et al., 2014; Ayata, 2011; Başer, 2015; Bruinessen, 1998; Demir, 2012; Eccarius-Kelly, 2002; Eliassi, 2013; Griffiths, 2000; Hassanpour and Mojab, 2004; Keles, 2015; Leggewie, 1996; Mahmod, 2016; Østergaard-Nielsen, 2001; Thangaraj, 2019; Toivanen and Başer, 2019; Wahlbeck, 1998). While acknowledging the importance of these works for our understanding of Kurdish diaspora, it is probably not unfair to say that few have contextualised Kurdish diaspora within a global context – for example, either through unpacking the interventions Kurdish diaspora have made to the Global North itself, or within the context of empire and coloniality. Yet it is not possible to understand the Kurdish movement and the Kurdish diaspora without understanding the role of the Ottoman, French and British empires, their consolidation of borders, their governance and population regimes and their negotiations with ethnic and religious alliances in the Middle East. Kurds' incorporation into the various nation-states that followed these empires is thus a postcolonial phenomenon. Approaches that focus solely on the nation-state have inevitably left out a consideration of the Kurdish diaspora using the insights of, for example, the Global South, decoloniality, postcoloniality or indigeneity. Instead, regional, nation-state and security-dominated perspectives continue to dominate the field, conceptualising Kurds as a minority group within respective states rather than as an indigenous group whose members question nation-centric conceptualisations and borders in the Middle East and in diaspora. Such absences are, in fact, not much different from those that can be identified in the numerous recent empirical studies of other diasporic groups, studies that have multiplied since the start of the millennium. The overwhelming majority of the works on diaspora have focused on particular case studies of a diasporic group (the Albanians, Indians, Palestinians, etc.). Such case studies have provided a detailed understanding of a particular diaspora and its trajectory, but less information on how the interventions made by diasporas to the global order, how they 'strike back', and whether and how they dislodge coloniality (Gilroy,

1993; Hall, 1990; Sivanandan, 1982). Diaspora theorising, on the whole, has remained focused on definitions and characteristics of diasporas or on hybridity. This book aims to shift the focus of diaspora studies from both of these theoretical positions, and instead discuss it in the context of colonialism, nationalism, race, empire, power and violence. The exigency and resolve of diaspora transpire in these contexts.

If diasporas are not to be simply seen as mediators or agents of their homeland politics, but as agents who speak back and challenge the Global North, then more attention needs to be paid to their translations, undoings of colonisation and unlearnings. Having provided examples of this from South Asian and Afro-Caribbean diasporas in the United Kingdom in the previous chapters, I will now turn to a discussion of my own empirical research on the Kurdish diaspora in this chapter. I will unpack how Kurdish diaspora carry out different types of ethno-political translations of their struggle[1] to two specific audiences: to other diasporic Kurds in Europe and to their non-Kurdish fellow European citizens. Such *translations* of ethno-political identity are central for the *transnational* and *decolonial* battles of Kurds. It is important to examine how and why, following the conceptualisation I offered in previous chapters, such diasporic translations are forms of rewriting, of undoing colonisation, and of both foreignising and domesticating. In my attempt to rethink the Kurdish diaspora globally, dislodging coloniality at home and in the new home, the chapter will also examine the Kurdish diaspora as 'transnational indigenous resistance', helping to develop an understanding of this diaspora not only globally, but also as inscribed in a series of historical and political processes associated with empire and expansion, including nationalist and other responses to these.

Kurdish diaspora in Europe

The Council of Europe Report of 2006 estimates that 25–30 million Kurds mainly live in four states, Iran, Iraq, Syria and Turkey, 'making them one of the largest "stateless nations" in the world' (Council of Europe, 2006). They are the fourth largest group in the Middle East after Arabs, Iranians and Turks. There are, however, no reliable official numbers or statistics on the number of Kurds. In 2017, the Kurdish Institute in Paris estimated them to range between 36.4 million (minimum estimate) and 45.6 million (maximum estimate). The BBC estimates that '25 and 35 million Kurds inhabit a mountainous region straddling the borders of Turkey, Iraq, Syria, Iran and Armenia' (BBC, 2019). However this last report excludes millions of Kurds living in cities such as Istanbul, Izmir, Mersin, Khorassan and Tehran. Kurds constitute approximately 20 per cent of the population of Turkey (15–20 million Kurds), 12.5 per cent of the population of Iran (10–12 million), 26 per cent of the population of Iraq (eight million) and 10 per cent of the population of Syria (three million) (Kurdish Institute, 2017). These numbers are rough and uncertain; their exact number is unknown due to official statistics not being available, census forms in respective states not collecting data on Kurdish ethnicity, and due to regional turmoil, such as the civil war in Syria. In Iraq there are more reliable numbers, yet even there the first census since 1997, which was due in 2020, has been postponed.

However, it is well established that largest number of Kurds live in Turkey, followed by Iran, Iraq and Syria, in the areas where the borders of these countries meet (North Kurdistan (Bakur), East Kurdistan (Rojhelat), Southern Kurdistan (Başûr) and West Kurdistan (Rojava)). Kurds also populate other cities and regions in these countries. For example, due to urbanisation, armed conflict and displacement, many Kurds also live in the 'western' parts of Turkey: Istanbul is the city with the largest Kurdish population in the world with an estimated three million Kurds (Bruinessen, 1998; Saraçoğlu, 2010). Some of the other largest Kurdish cities are Diyarbakır, Urfa, Antep (in Turkey), Kermanchah and Sinneh (in Iran), Suleimaniah, Kirkuk, Duhok (in Iraq), Afrin, Quamishli and Kobane (in Syria).

Kurds also make up a sizeable proportion of Europe's ethnic minority population. According to an estimation in 2006, there were more than one million Kurds living in Europe (Council of Europe, 2006), although the International Crisis Group Report (2012) estimates that between 1 and 1.5 million Kurds from Turkey live in Europe, signalling that the total number of Kurds in Europe, including from other countries, is much bigger. This also tallies with a more recent estimate from 2016, which says there are 1.5 million

Kurds living mainly in Western Europe (Kurdish Institute, 2017). The total number of Kurds in particular European states is inevitably a rough estimation due to many European states recording the country of origin but not ethnic background in their official documents and census. The estimates are: 850,000–950,000 in Germany; 230,000–250,000 in France; and 100,000–120,000 in the Netherlands (Kurdish Institute, 2016). In France, for example, the census collects information about nationality at birth and current nationality. Data on ethnicity are not officially collected in the French census or by other official means. In fact, it is forbidden by law to collect data on racial or ethnic origin. This not only makes it impossible to find out data on Kurds (and other minorities) in France, but also makes structural discrimination difficult to identify (Gilbert and Keane, 2016). In France, data are collected based on the country of origin – that is, on 'foreigners' and 'immigrants' – (Institut National d'Etudes Démographiques, 2020). In Germany, the only census conducted since the reunification in 1990 took place in 2011. However, that census did not collect data on ethnicity either. In the Netherlands, government statistics follow a similar route and collect data on nationality and country of origin rather than ethnicity. Such colour-blind census methods by European states mean that we do not have census data on Kurds or reliable numbers for other ethnic minorities in Europe. By recording country of origin of immigrants but not their ethnicity or the ethnicity of their own citizens, the structural discrimination and exclusions faced by many ethnic minorities in Europe go unidentified. Individual discrimination is also difficult to prosecute, as it relies on the penal code rather than the civil code, demanding a much higher burden of proof. Additionally, the focus on the country of origin does not allow the life trajectories of those from different racial and ethnic backgrounds, but from the same country of origin, to be identified. These often go undetected. Some of the problems faced by Kurds and Turks from Turkey living in Europe, are different, for example. The former's persecuted exclusion and marginalised status brought from home impact their life chances and their politics in diaspora. Yet European states are unable to identify issues specific to ethnic groups as they collect data on 'the country of origin' and ignore ethnicity. In so doing, European states are inadvertently reproducing the erasure that Kurds (and other minoritised groups) have had to endure previously in their countries of origin. This methodological nationalism and colour-blindness of many European census forms has profound consequences.

The UK census is an exception. It allows respondents to record their ethnicity. The number of Kurds in the United Kingdom was identified as 49,841 in the 2011 census. How much this number under-estimates the real number has been ridiculed – as I and others have often repeated in London, 'If there are so few Kurds in the United Kingdom, I must know them all!' There are many reasons for this outcome of the 2011 census in the United Kingdom. In the 2011 census, Kurdish was not one of the predefined boxes for the ethnicity, requiring Kurds to tick 'other' and write down their ethnicity. Due to the assimilation policies at home, Kurds are used to categorising themselves as 'Turkish' or 'Iranian', especially when dealing with officialdom. It should come as no surprise that many may not have entered 'Kurdish' in the 2011 UK census, similar to the way in which Alevi children are likely to be registered as Muslim or having no religion by their parents when dealing with officialdom (Jenkins, 2020; Jenkins and Cetin, 2017). Additionally, we must remember that some Kurds, like other new arrivals, have had informal living, work and even settlement arrangements, so are more likely to fall through the gaps and not be recorded. In the United States, the 'Kurds Count' campaign is encouraging Kurds to fill out the census by putting 'Kurdish' in the race question. There was a similar UK campaign to get Kurds counted in the 2011 census. There might be renewed demands that 'Kurdish' is included as one of the predefined boxes in a future UK census. Other official documents and data on Kurds in the United Kingdom – for example, the Home Office data – are also insufficient. When the bulk of Kurds arrived in the United Kingdom as asylum seekers in the late 1980s and 1990s, the Home Office only recorded their country of origin, not their ethnicity. Kurds have remained invisible due to such practices (King et al., 2008). Despite the British practice of recording ethnic origin in the census, we still do not have accurate numbers – at least for Kurds. We have to rely on estimates in the United Kingdom as in the rest of Europe. Nevertheless, we know there is a sizeable Kurdish population; it is estimated that between one million and 1.5 million Kurds live in Europe.

The presence of Kurds in Europe is not recent. Kurds have been in Europe for many decades, but especially from the 1960s onwards. The first wave of Kurds arrived from Turkey as *Gastarbeiter* (guest workers) following a 'labour agreement' signed between Turkey and the then 'West' Germany, but many also arrived as immigrant workers to Austria, Switzerland, France and the Benelux countries. Kurdish intellectuals and students also came in this period. The second wave of Kurds came to European cities, escaping violence and oppression, in the 1980s and 1990s. For example, many arrived from Iran before and following the Islamic Revolution in 1979 and from Turkey following the 1980 coup and especially during the 1990s, when faced with suppression and violence. Other Kurds came escaping the Anfal[2] extermination campaign against the Kurds in 1980s and also as a result of the inter-Kurdish clashes in Iraqi Kurdistan in the 1990s. The impetus for Kurds' move to Europe was brought about by assimilationist and repressive policies, displacement and facing interrelated political, economic and social exclusions in countries such as Iraq, Iran and Turkey (e.g. see Allison, 2016; Bayır, 2013; Bozarslan, 2001; Gündoğan, 2011; Houston, 2004; Human Rights Watch, 2010, 2012; Saraçoğlu, 2010; Vali, 2014; Zeydanlıoğlu, 2008). In Turkey, for example, as a result of the armed conflict between the Turkish army and the Kurdistan Workers' Party (PKK), many thousands lost their lives and many thousands more were forcibly removed and displaced.[3] Members of Kurdish parties and supporters faced 'extra-legal threats' and 'extra-judicial killings' (Watts, 2010: 109–10) and extensive coercion and torture (White, 2007; Zeydanlıoğlu, 2009). In this period, thousands of Kurdish villages were evacuated (Human Rights Watch, 2010) and more than 40,000 people died as a result of the violence.[4] Since around 2011, Syrian Kurds arrived in Europe, mainly in Germany, as part of the flood of Syrian refugees fleeing the violence and war in Syria (Ostrand, 2015; Şimşek, 2017).

While these push factors are important for understanding part of the story of why Kurds have moved to Europe, they leave unaccounted the history of colonisation, expansion and retraction of empires in the region – not only Kurds' subordination, but also their agency in dealing with these powers, including their negotiations, rebellions and struggles in order to regain or retain their autonomy through the centuries (e.g. Özok-Gündoğan, 2014). It is not possible to understand Kurdish diaspora without understanding the role of the Ottoman, French and British empires, their subordination, colonisation, expansion, retraction and bordering. These empires have consolidated populations and religious and ethnic alliances in the Middle East and have reorganised borders in the region, making Kurds a minoritised group. A recognition of this brings us closer to understanding why I conceptualise the Kurdish diaspora as an example of 'transnational indigeneity' rather than limiting understandings of them to 'ethno-political' struggles and violence within nation-states.

Not just numerically but also in terms of political activism and mobilisation, the Kurdish presence in Europe has been strong, and proliferating. Kurds now constitute a significant proportion of diasporic groups in European capitals such as Berlin, Paris, London and Stockholm, but also in other European cities such as Sheffield (UK), Strasbourg (France), Hannover (Germany), Rotterdam (Netherlands), Basel (Switzerland) and others. They have created a vibrant political space in Europe, are active in the politics of the countries in which they have settled, and continue their translations of Kurdish identity, culture and politics. Kurds became possibly the 'best-organised diasporic community in Europe' (Arslan, 2005). Until the 1980s, Kurdish politics in Europe was mainly, although not exclusively, leftist and revolved around fighting against class and tribal privileges. After the late 1980s, there was a shift towards diaspora politics becoming Kurdish-oriented. The suppression of Kurds' political, cultural and linguistic rights, alongside the upsurge of ethno-politically mobilised Kurds in diaspora in the late 1980s and 1990s, reoriented diaspora politics. Many diasporic organisations became Kurdish-focused and began to have the Kurdish struggle as a central concern; some of their members began to feel allegiance to the cause of the Kurdish movement, which is composed of a variety of actors, including the PKK. The PKK is listed as a terrorist organisation by Turkey, the European Union and the United States, but diaspora politics nevertheless subsumed it (International Crisis Group Report, 2012). Many Kurds – even rival Kurdish organisations – recognise the PKK's hegemonic position in the mobilisation of the Kurdish diaspora, which Soguk (2008: 182) calls the 'sublime politics' of the PKK. The Anfal genocide and the wars in Iraq exposed the ongoing oppression, as well as possibilities for autonomy, and further galvanised the diasporic Kurds. Following the imprisonment of Öcalan (the leader of the PKK) in 1999, and village evacuations, the Kurdish movement in Turkey over time became an urban movement. After a period of 'Kurdish opening', peace talks (2013–15) and ceasefire, political oppression and violence have intensified in Turkey since 2015 (Gunes, 2017, 2019; Martin, 2018).[5] These, together with the referendum in Iraqi Kurdistan and the Kurdish fight against ISIS in Rojava, have fired up diasporic Kurdish politics again since 2015. Outrage against the suppression of Kurds and violence in the Middle East continues to incite Kurdish diasporic activism. Leggewie (1996) argues that, in Germany, many self-identified 'Turks' became self-identified 'Kurds', not self-identified 'Germans'. I argue that amongst Kurds there was also a shift from being a migrant, a shift from being concerned with adaptation to the new home and a shift from dealing with everyday social and economic problems to a diasporic consciousness, diasporic practices and mobilisation towards impacting politics in Europe (Demir, 2017a). Over time, some of those who were refugees and migrants from Iran, Iraq and Turkey became part of the 'Kurdish diaspora' in Europe.

Methods

Like other groups, of course, Kurds in Europe are not homogeneous. There are significant differences in religiosity, educational levels, language, class positions, sectarian allegiances and political stances. Kurds' strategies and possibilities for engaging with Europe and their homeland ties and struggles vary. Moreover, there are also differences in terms of languages spoken, the media followed and the affinities created, depending on their country of origin and the part of Kurdistan from which they originate. Political divisions exist: 'The collective memorialisation and commemoration of Ocalan among North Kurdistanis [do] not operate equivalently across Kurdistan or ... within the many Kurdish diasporas' (Thangaraj, 2019: 3). There is a vibrant Kurdish political space in Europe aimed at dislodging coloniality. The Kurdish diaspora proactively translate Kurdish struggles, identity, culture and politics to other Kurds, especially to their newer generations and other non-political Kurds, and to other citizens and inhabitants of Europe.

In order to examine how diasporic Kurds translate Kurdish identity, culture and struggle to others, I carried out one-to-one, semi-structured interviews with 122 Kurds. I attempted to speak to Kurds who actively revived, constructed, maintained and translated to others. Recruitment was facilitated through collaborations with existing connections from previous research and various Kurdish community networks. I used snowball sampling to recruit more participants and spoke to Kurds living in Sheffield, Leicester, London, Paris, Cologne and Berlin. Due to issues of proximity to the researcher, most of the interviewees took place with Kurds who live in the United Kingdom. Some of the findings from the earlier phases of this research were published and have identified, for example, how Kurds undertake 'ethno-political tuition' and 'ethnic entrepreneurial labouring' in diaspora (Demir, 2015); Kurdish diasporic cosmopolitanism (Demir, 2016); de-Turkification strategies of Kurdish diaspora (Demir, 2017a); Kurdish diaspora as the Global South in the Global North (Demir, 2017b); and Kurdish transnational indigeneity (Demir, 2021). My discussion below in this phase of the research turns attention to issues of rewriting, of undoing colonisation and of both foreignising and domesticating in diaspora.

As discussed above, Kurds – like any ethnic group – are not homogeneous. The research and arguments underpinning this chapter examine the translational activities of the Kurdish diaspora by focusing on Kurds who originate from Turkey (80) though Kurds from Iran (18), Iraq (19) and Syria (5) also participated. This is not unwarranted. Amir Hassanpour and Shahrzad Mojab (2004) underline that, not just in terms of numbers but also in terms of activism, diasporic Kurds originating from Turkey lead the way. Natali (2005) notes that Iranian Kurdish diaspora are less mobilised. However, this is relative and should be seen in the context of Kurds being often highly absorbed in the future of Kurdistan and Kurdishness.

Interviews attempted to uncover how the Kurdish struggle was translated to non-Kurdish (especially to the host community) and Kurdish audiences (especially to newer generations of Kurds born and raised in Europe). I asked questions such as, 'Where do you

say you are from when a British person[6] – let's say at a social event
– asks?'; 'How do you learn more about the Kurdish struggle? From
whom? Who or what inspired you?'; 'Do you interrupt or correct
other Kurds if you disagree with them about the Kurdish issue? Can
you give me an example?'; 'How do you convey the Kurdish story
to the British? What do you share? Do you refrain from telling anything? Can you give me an example?'; 'How do you inform others
about the Kurds in Iran – for example, the Republic of Kurdistan
in Mahabad?'; 'Do you tell the British about their involvement?
How do you tell them and how is it received?'; 'How do newer
generations of Kurds in Europe find out about the Anfal genocide?
How is it passed on?'; and 'Is there anything you were taught back
at home about Kurds that you learnt to question or unlearn in
Berlin?'.

Through questions such as these and others, I attempted to
uncover not only how Kurds translate and decolonise, but why
they do so in particular ways. Participants were asked to discuss times when they had to correct and interrupt their newer
generations, other Kurds and the host community. Asking them
to think of their own (anonymised) examples provided much rich
data. Issues relating to the particular activities of Kurdish diasporic
organisations or their relationship to the Kurdish movement were
not investigated. Instead, how Kurds translated Kurdish identity
and struggle was explored. I paid special attention to interviewing
Kurds from different political perspectives, genders, religious and
sectarian backgrounds. Kurdish women are especially vocal, and
also in positions of power in diaspora politics (Cockburn, 2017). In
my sample of 122 for this research, a majority (73) were women.
Interviews usually lasted about an hour. In addition to formal
interviews, I talked to many members of the Kurdish community,
and undertook observations during various public demonstrations,
meetings and festivals. I also examined publicly available news
pieces from diasporic media, documents and Kurdish community
association publications and websites as part of the 'grey literature'.
The study fully adhered to university ethical guidelines and the
Code of Ethics of the British Sociological Association. Data were
anonymised and all potentially identifiable data were removed.

When examining the data, Timmermans and Tavory's (2012)
abductive analysis was employed. This helped to overcome the

limitations of solely relying on deduction or induction. It enabled surprising findings and patterns to emerge and encouraged theoretical innovation. When analysing the data, techniques and strategies such as coding, memo writing and constant comparison from grounded theory were also used. Saturation was reached when no new themes were identified. Emergent themes and trends that addressed rewriting, translation and decolonisation were identified. When providing examples in the findings below, those interviews that were held in a language other than English were translated, with the original retained next to the quote below.

Rewriting, domesticating and foreignising: Translating the Kurdish struggle

Salvaging and translation of an ethno-political identity in diaspora is neither easy nor effortless. Translation of identity in diaspora involves negotiation and rendering of identity and of history, the reshaping and retelling of collective memory, strategies of inclusion and exclusion, and gatekeeping, never mind thinking about audiences and to whom to say what. Such salvaging and translation become all the more important if an ethno-political identity – like being Kurdish – does not have a nation-state that purports to represent it. It gets even more complicated when, as a minoritised group, the group in discussion has been subject to oppression, subjugation and erasure at home. It becomes yet further difficult if the host community's knowledge of them is minimal, despite their (as in the case of the United Kingdom, France and the United States) central role in the reorganisation of the borders in the Middle East, and the dividing up and bordering of Kurdistan in the twentieth and twenty-first centuries.[7]

In my research, I identified that the Kurdish struggle is translated to two main groups, and how it is translated is different. The Kurdish struggle is translated to the European audiences in an informative way, telling it in a way that deploys human rights language. It focuses on the suffering faced by Kurds. To the newer generations, however, the translations use emotive language, based on attempting to galvanise the newer generations of Kurdish youth in Europe. For example:

Germany, France etc. they have human rights. When it is explained in that language, they understand. Our plight is one of human rights too. *[Almanya, Fransa falan bunlarda insan hakları var. O dilden anlatınca anlıyorlar. Zaten mücadelemiz de esas olarak insan hakları mücadelesidir].*

(Male, 52)

Europeans know about the Anfal genocide in Iraq. They know the genocidal campaign of Saddam Hussein. I start there and tell my own family's history of being poisoned. I don't do too much victimhood though. They stop listening.

(Female, 49)

We of course can't explain it to the Europeans in the language of the mountains [referring to the Kurdish guerrillas]. *[Kalkıp Avrupalılara dağ dilinde anlatacak halimiz yok].*

(Female, 44)

So what do I say to others about Kurds? Hmm ... I don't know, I was never ashamed of my Kurdishness. So what I say is ... we are not asking for charity or for special treatment. We don't want to be tortured and oppressed for asking for our rights. I would give my life to a Turk who is not racist or fascist. That's the message I give to Europeans. *[Söylediklerim mi? ... Ne bileyim, mesela ben Kürtlüğümden hiç utanmadım. Söylediğim işte ... zaten biz kimseden yardım veya ayrıcalık talep etmiyoruz. Hakkımızı istiyoruz diye zulüm ve baskı görmek istemiyoruz. Irkçı faşist olmayan Türk'e canım feda. Avrupa'ya verdiğim mesaj işte budur].*

(Male, 55)

On the whole, translations to other European citizens were couched in the language of rights and suffering. The translations were thus, if we apply Venuti's concept, 'domesticated' (Venuti, 1995). This is not to say that Europeans never heard the rebellion story. Nor does it mean that newer generations of Kurds did not hear about suffering from their parents – they did. However, what distinguished translations for newer generations of Kurds was their amplified foreignising translation of 'dignity', 'rebellion' and 'uprising' of an oppressed indigenous population. When I asked about a picture of Lady Diana placed next to a Kurdish rebellion leader on a mantle-piece in the United Kingdom, I was told 'I love them both, right next to one another; they both rebelled' (Female, 58). Many other participants also underlined rebellion – for example:

My children, I want them to fill up with emotion when I say 'we the Kurds'. I tell them of the struggle in Iraq and in Turkey, of our rebellions. If I knew more about the struggle in Iran, I'd tell them that too.

(Male, 32)

I especially emphasise we are the indigenous owners of those lands. We are a substantive component, not a mere minority. We resisted. There is even a name 'Resistance'. I always underline this when talking to our youth. *[Hatta biz o toprakların en kadim sahipleriyiz. Asli unsuruz, azınlık değiliz. Baskıya direndik yüzyıllarca. Diren diye isim bile var. Hep bunun altını çiziyorum gençlere.]*

(Female, 45)

If mum and dad had a fight at home, my mum would shame my father by saying, 'if you suppress like the Turkish state, I will rise up like the Kurds'. *[Annemle babam kavga ederse, annem hep 'Türk devleti gibi baskı yaparsan, Kürtler gibi ayaklanırım bak' deyip babamı utandırırdı, dize getirirdi.]*

(Female, 30)

We are *serhildan*. That's the Kurdish identity passed onto us.

(Female, 24)[8]

It is well known that music has been an important aspect of retaining and passing on Kurdishness and articulating resistance. *Koms* (Kurdish music groups) have contributed to the construction and shaping of Kurdish identity in the 1990s and beyond (Sarıtaş, 2010). Translations of Kurdishness via culture in diaspora occurred via the social practices, revolutionary songs and stories. Kurdish films and novels reflected these too (Hussain, 2020). Even Kurdish food and Kurdish dancing (*govend*) could be conceptualised and thus passed on as part of the struggle to other Kurds and newer generations. For example:

My cousins [who live in Brussels] and I speak in broken Kurdish and Turkish. They don't speak English well; I don't speak French. But we excel at Kurdish dancing. *[Bizim kuzenler Brükselde. Aramızda çat pat Türkce, Kürtçe konuşuruz. Onların İngilizcesi pek iyi değil. Benim de Fransızcam. Ama halayda döktürürüz.]* [comment followed by laughter]

(Female, 32)

Continuing to cook Kurdish food is part of our struggle, part of keeping our culture. It is not just *kebap*. We are going to make our Kurdish *dolma* [referring to a dish of stuffed vegetables] world famous. Whoever eats it will get to know Kurds.

(Female, 54)

My children grew up in Germany with me frying onions and paste on the stove. I was banging on the pot and singing Kurdish revolutionary songs with the *komas* [Kurdish resistance musicians], Perwers [Kurdish musician]. That's how they got injected [with the Kurdish struggle]. *[Ve çocuklar benim soğanla salçayi tencerede şöyle kavura kuvura çevirirken söylediğim Kürtçe müzikle, komalarla, Perwerlerle büyüdü Almanya'da. İçlerine işledi. Öyle bulaştı.]*

(Female, 50)

Yet it was not always possible to foreignise the newer generations, and domesticate the message to the Europeans. Misunderstanding European sensitivities, misreading younger Kurds and miscalculating other Kurds' views of the Kurdish struggle also occurred. Such stories were commonly brought up, if asked about:

A friend had brought her German boyfriend to a charity event for Heyva Sor [Kurdish Red Moon]. When leaving, the boyfriend was terrified. They were wearing guerrilla clothing, asking for donations!

(Female, 33)

My uncle's love of guerrillas made me grow colder [to the Kurdish struggle]. His propandising made me grow colder. *[Dayımın gerilla aşkı beni soğuttu vallahi. Propaganda soğuttu.]*

(Male, 22)

They did this stand-up comedy event to raise funds but then overdid the victim and pity bit in the middle.

(Male, 46)

In the interviews, I identified how the same story was told to both the newer generations of Kurds in Europe and to non-Kurds in Europe. One of these revolved around drawing comparisons between the treatment of Black people in apartheid South Africa and that of Kurds in Turkey, and also between the PKK leader Abdullah Öcalan and Nelson Mandela. Mandela became an ally of the Kurdish struggle in the 1990s. He in fact compared Kurds with the way Black Africans were oppressed in South Africa under apartheid. In 1992, he turned down the Ataturk Peace Prize from

Turkey. Later in 1997, at a Kurdish festival in Germany, he sent a message to Kurds supporting their plight, going so far as to say, 'I am part of the Kurdish struggle. I am one of you' (Mandela, 1997). He became an important international figure for Kurds. A majority of my interviewees who were older remembered his support vividly, and reported bringing up Mandela's support for the Kurdish struggle in their interactions often, not just with non-Kurds but also with the Kurdish youth:

> Mandela turned down the peace prize from Turkey. He sent solidarity messages to us Kurds in Germany. I speak of this a lot, for example. *[Mandela Türkiye'den gelen barış ödülünü reddetti. Almanya'da biz Kürtlere yoldaşız mesajı yolladı. Bunu hep diyorum mesela].*
> (Female, 52)

> They put pictures of Mandela and Apo [referring to Öcalan] [on flags] when off to Trafalgar Square for demonstrations. Who are these for? So Europeans see it. *[Mandela ile Apo resimleri koyuyorlar [bayraklara] gösteriye çıkarken. Avrupalılar görsün diye tabii..]*
> (Male, 48)

A comparison between Kurdish suffering and Irish suffering under British colonialism was also drawn by my interviewees when domesticating the Kurdish struggle for non-Kurds. Such comparisons were reported as increasing the sympathies of Europeans towards the Kurds, and also enrolling the newer generations of Kurds into Kurdishness:

> Even Britain did not wipe out whole neighbourhoods of Belfast in order to fight the IRA. Yet Turkey wiped out Sur [a neighbourhood of Diyarbakır]. I was school age when they signed the peace treaty [Good Friday Agreement]. I remember it distinctly. My father said to our Irish neighbours that we want the same thing ... I think the neighbours had never thought about the similarity between us and them [the Irish] before. Making a connection through their traumas was important.
> (Female, 35)

> Our youth learn it at school and draw a comparison between the English oppression in Ireland and what Kurds are going through. *[Gençlerimiz okulda öğreniyorlar, parallellik kuruyorlar İrlandadaki İngiliz baskısı ile Kürtlerin yaşadıkları arasında.]*
> (Male, 42)

In addition to comparisons with Mandela and the Irish, the increase in the attention paid by the rest of the world to the Rojava conflict and to the female Kurdish guerrillas fighting ISIS in Syria were reported as being energising by my interviewees. The utopian, ecological and gendered angles of the 'Rojava Revolution' were reported as being highly effective in energising the newer generations of the Kurdish diaspora. They were also reported to have drawn volunteers who were poised to fight against ISIS. The 'Rojava Revolution' both gendered and transnationalised the Kurdish struggle. What about for non-Kurds? Overall, the interviews showed that the 'Rojava Revolution' both foreignised and domesticated the Kurdish struggle. The gender angle of the 'Rojava Revolution' helped to domesticate it for non-Kurdish audiences, rewriting it in the world-view of the receiving culture. Translations focusing on gender elevated and rendered the struggle in the world-view of the European receiver. The women were fighting injustice and patriarchy, and together with the violence of ISIS helped to make the Kurdish struggle not just agreeable to Europeans, but also immediately relatable. For example:

> When we tried to explain about Kurdish women's equality struggle and wins to women's organisations in Berlin, there was much interest from Germans. They became interested in Kurds more and we told them more.
>
> (Female, 37)

> France has had a long history with Syria and the Kurds – it was their mandate. But the fight women put up in Rojava gained us much sympathy in France. *[Fransa'nın zaten Kürtlerle, Suriye ile bağı var, eski mandası. Ama Rojavadaki kadınların savaşımı çok sempati kazandırdı Fransa'da.]*
>
> (Female, 26)

> Europe has now got to know Kurdish women. We could fight ISIS in [YPJ] uniforms but also wear our cultural clothing. Europe even copied our women's fashion ...
>
> (Female, 38)[9]

> You see, even *Marie Claire* liked it ... [*Marie Claire'in bile hoşuna gitmiş baksana ...*]
>
> (Female, 24)[10]

The utopian angle of the 'Rojava Revolution', on the other hand, foreignised the Kurdish struggle for non-Kurds. I was able to identify that non-Kurds' expectations were not always pandered to, and moments of 'not understanding' existed. Some of these disparities were turned into what White (1995: 338) calls 'spaces for learning', an invitation to go beyond and learn. However, even though such foreignising translations refused erasure through smoothing, a 'compensation approach' (Tymoczko, 2007) was often employed alongside foreignisation – that is, differences, misunderstandings and disparities were offset via further explanations and background about the Kurdish struggle.

So far, I have provided a discussion of some of the translational practices of the Kurdish diaspora, including how it was rewritten but also foreignised and domesticated in translations. As shown, the discourse of 'dignity', 'rebellion' and 'uprising' of an oppressed indigenous population was dominant in the translations of the Kurdish struggle to newer generations of Kurds in diaspora. The Kurdish struggle was told to Europeans in a way that deployed human rights language, focusing on the suffering faced by Kurds. To their own community, Kurds were presented as 'agents' and as 'doers', whereas to the European audiences, Kurds were more likely to be presented as 'victims'. Kurdish guerrillas who died during the clashes with the army were presented as martyrs, not as victims, to the newer generations. The pictures and stories about them were conveyed as stories of dignity to newer generations. It was possible to identify that, despite some exceptions, for the Europeans most of the translations 'domesticated' the Kurdish struggle and foreignised only some aspects, and most translations to the newer generations were mostly foreignising, telling a story of rebellion and uprising. Yet certain stories – for example, Mandela's support for Kurds – were drawn on in translations to both groups.

It is important that these two types of translations – that is, foreignising and domesticating translations of the Kurdish struggle – should not be seen as mischievousness or a type of contradiction on the part of a diaspora. A struggle can have both a human rights angle and a rebellion angle. There can be both dignity and victimhood. That we would expect one dimension to any identity or struggle would be an analyst's fallacy, a poor sociological understanding of any struggle and identity. Additionally, that an identity or struggle is presented in the same language, as a uniform and standardised story to all audiences, is perhaps a relic of essentialist understanding of identity. Neither Kurds nor their reception of the Kurdish struggle can be seen as homogeneous. That we present and explain different sides of ourselves to different people is an unavoidable and enriching aspect of human life. We do not talk to our lovers in the same language we use to talk to our friends. We would talk to our bosses differently from how we talk to our relatives, even about the same topic. Hence, instead of presenting these two types of translations as a duality or duplicity on the side of diasporas, we must look back and question our analyst position. Why are we expecting a unidimensional narrative? Are we reading contradiction where none is present? Indeed, Kurds do not see a contradiction between these different sides of their struggle. This is why, even though I identified different types of translation, I did not present this as an inconsistency or duplicity on the part of actors.

Similarly, the issue of rewriting must be tackled head on. I argued that through such rewritings, the Kurdish story was made plausible, digestible and palatable for European audiences; it was also able to enrol newer generations to Kurdishness. Nor should this notion of rewriting during translation be approached as an inconsistency or as part of a cunning plan. The process of translating always involves selection – an appraisal. Through telling of the Kurdish story to newer generations by centring it on stories of dignity, rebellion and uprising, and glossing over other stories, the Kurdish struggle is also rewritten in diaspora. As discussed in Chapter 2, rewriting in any translation is unavoidable. There is always indeterminacy and rewriting involved in translating and retelling a struggle. That diasporas rewrite is hence unsurprising. Any translator uses judgement to assess differences and rewrite; diasporas can introduce newness, shift meaning and focus through their rewriting. It is rather how diasporas rewrite, what they leave out, what they foreignise and what they domesticate that need discovering, identifying and unpacking. I carried this out in relation to the Kurdish diaspora in Europe. Just as Benjamin (1968) highlights the translator's task in renewal and transformation, we must investigate the role of diasporas in retelling in order to identify how diasporas can mould the contours of their new identity and challenge prescriptive identities brought from home or imposed on them in the new home.

Such forms of rewriting undertaken by diasporas can only be approached suspiciously if simplistic notions of authenticity are allowed to dominate. First, a wider acknowledgement of diasporic rewriting can in fact challenge the futility of our craving for authenticity. This is a salient point for the field of Kurdish studies as well as for diaspora studies. Second, such a rewriting should enable us to jettison the often-repeated, yet analytically rather dull, 'in-betweenness of diaspora'. Diaspora studies and empirical research on diaspora are far too often captured in this kind of language – that is, diaspora conceived of as an entity squeezed in between two existing forms, if not lost and falling through the gaps between cultures. Only essentialised understandings of culture can construct diasporas as hemmed in and crushed between two cultures and nations, ignoring existing gaps and divisions within a culture, an ethnic group or a nation. A refined understanding of translation, which acknowledges the rewriting involved in any translation, can help to challenge the pointless craving for authenticity and the binary world-view in which the field of diaspora studies is sometimes trapped. Every translation is a rewriting and, instead of a binary between a receiver and an originator, we should look out for, and make indispensable, the multiplicity of translations and world-views of diasporas. Last but not least, rewriting should not be approached negatively but as a way in which diasporas can intervene in and shape the culture and debates in the new home, back home and globally. Rewriting, foreignising and domesticating are means through which diasporas intervene, aid decolonisation and leave a mark.

Undoing colonisation in diaspora: Kurdish transnational indigenous resistance

Kurdish peoples continue to pursue greater rights and autonomy throughout Kurdistan. They have also inspired and mobilised diaspora politics. In the case of Kurds, it was mobilisations in Kurdistan that initially cultivated and inspired a Kurdish diaspora, not the other way around. Yet increasingly we are seeing that such efforts are now being amplified via the transnationalisation of the Kurdish issue by the Kurdish diaspora, especially since the arrival of politicised Kurds in Europe. The Kurdish diaspora, through both translations to newer generations of Kurds in Europe and to Europeans directly, is able to challenge Orientalised and colonial knowledges about Kurds both in the new home and in the homes left behind. I refer to this process of challenging knowledges as 'undoing colonisation in diaspora'.

While it is true that there is no one narrative and translation, diasporic Kurds question certain standard views and knowledges about themselves. The research identified three central ways in which undoings of colonisation occur. First, it occurs through epistemic interventions – that is, through identifying, recalling and retelling what was, and still is, erased. A standard example is colonial map-making and Kurds ending up as minoritised populations in four different countries. Kurdish lands were carved up in the first half of the twentieth century between the British, French and Turkish rule. Colonial arrangements and a series of mandates put Syria and Lebanon under French rule, and Iraq, Transjordan and Palestine under British rule, dividing Kurds across different countries and zones of control. Such carving up of lands showed little regard for the religious, ethnic or sectarian characteristics of the area. There is thus a close link between Kurds becoming minoritised populations and map-making and bordering of the Middle East through colonial interventions. The Kurdish diaspora links the current predicament of Kurds to the history of imperialism and colonialism, and to indigenous identities and discourses (e.g. *asli unsur*; *kadim sahip*). This is why I conceptualise Kurdish diaspora as an example of 'transnational indigeneity' rather than limit understandings of them to 'ethno-political' struggles and violence within nation-states, and consequent push factors.

Besides the carving up of Kurdish lands in early twentieth century, there is also the support given to the oppressive regimes throughout the twentieth century in the region – not just politically, but also militarily. This has been an ongoing issue highlighted by the Kurdish diaspora. From the 1920s, when there was a British air bombing campaign in Iraq to quell the uprising of Kurds and Arabs against the British – their colonial rulers – to the selling of arms and poison by the West (Germany, the United States and the

United Kingdom), which was used to launch a genocidal poisoning campaign against Kurds in 1988, to the selling of tanks to Turkey by Germany which were used against protestors, Kurds highlight the colonial suppressions they faced in the rest of the twentieth century. They echo the "we are here because you were there" sentiment that other postcolonial diasporas have deployed, making a link between the colonial history of Kurdistan and Kurds' presence in Europe today.

Diasporic Kurds are also challenging the knowledges created about them by the countries of the region. For example, they resist and refuse the construction of the Kurdish issue in Turkey, and by Turkey to Europe, primarily as a case of terrorism. They question stories that reduce the Kurdish issue to regional inequalities, and those that ignore colonial disinvestment and exploitation over centuries. They reject the perennial characterisation of the Kurdish issue as one of pre-modernity, backwardness and refusal to assimilate into civilisation and modernity. Instead, they seek to present various episodes of uprising and violence as an uprising against a colonial master. They often remember rebellions and violent episodes – for example:

> We did not forget Ağrı, Koçgiri, Dersim, Sivas, Çorum, Maraş, Halepçe, Anfal, Roboski. One after the other ... [*Ağrı, Koçgiri, Dersim, Sivas, Çorum, Maraş, Halabja, Enfal, Roboski'yi unutmadık. Bu böyle dizi dizi ...*]

> (Male, 52)

Second, trivialising knowledges and discourses created and reproduced about them back home were also challenged. Trivialisation via discursive strategies has often been employed in the context of colonisation to 'sweeten the horror or banalize' (Trouillot, 1995: 97). In the case of Kurds, that Kurds broke the Muslim brotherhood with Arabs and Turks, that there is equal citizenship for them, that many other non-Kurdish groups were also oppressed, that Kurds and Turks have always been brothers were often seen as trivial interjections and thus challenged:

> We are also sick of this brotherhood discourse. What kind of brotherhood is this? That they are the older brother ordering around, and we the little one expected to get in line to take orders? [*Bu kardeşlik*

söyleminden de bıktık. Ne biçim kardeşlik bu? Onlar abi, biz hazırola geçmesi gereken küçük kardeş ...]

(Male, 38)

They say that leftist Iranians were also suppressed [besides Kurds in Iran]. Yes but they were because they were politically on the left, not because they were Kurdish.

(Male, 58)

When we say we are Kurdish we are accused of being separatist. Yet the Turkish state in official declarations call Turks in Bulgaria and Central Asia 'our blood relatives'. Then they tell us Turkishness is a [civic] citizenship. How is it supposed to include us? It's obvious they mean ethnic kin when they say 'Turkish'. *[Kürdüz deyince biz ayırımcı oluyormuşuz. Türk devleti Bulgaristan'daki, Orta Asya'daki Türklere resmi ağızla 'canım soydaşlarımız' diyor. Hani Türklük vatandaşlıktı? Hani bizi de kapsıyordu? Kafasındaki Türklük soymus demek ki.]*

(Male, 49)

Third, undoing colonisation involves unlearning (Asad and Dixon, 1985: 173). Subverting hegemonic discourses include correcting Orientalist depictions of Kurds, implicit biases in language and perspective, and received understandings of gender relations. It happens through putting up a struggle against the reproduction of an Orientalist depiction of Kurds when others deploy it. Such narratives through state discourses and the media have shaped the ways in which Kurds and the Kurdish issue were understood in the Middle East, but also in Europe. Recently the Kurdish women's fight against ISIS was deployed to challenge customary and taken-for-granted views on both the Kurdish resistance and gender in the Middle East. Kurdish resistance and women's central role in it were framed in a way that pierced received Orientalist views and knowledges:

Finally they got to know the Kurdish women's movement. They were educated.

(Female, 28)

Even if we don't always talk about this [face to face, as much as we would like], on Twitter, Kurds and Kurdish struggle is out there.

European youth respect and follow the Rojava struggle. They are
attracted to this new revolutionary story of Kurds.

(Male, 36)

Such corrections were geared to challenge the received knowledges
of the Kurdish resistance and of gender and oppression in the
Middle East – knowledges that typically have been constitutive of
the North's framing of the region. They have also allowed the diaspora to intervene and expand the horizons of Europe. If, as Levander
and Mignolo (2011) argue, the Global South is not a geography,
but rather a case of demanding decoloniality, the Kurdish diaspora
should be understood as part of the Global South in the Global
North (Demir, 2017b) and as transnational indigenous resistance.

Of course, many other indigenous groups inhabit the Middle
East. A significant number of them have been at the receiving end of
various regional, national and global conflicts. Especially since the
beginning of the twentieth century, Armenians, Assyrians, Kurds,
Yezidis and many others have been subjected to regional conflicts
and state violence. This is not specific to the Middle East. There is
a close relationship between modernity and violence, and between
nationalism and violence. Yet in political, media and human rights
discourses, or in academia, analyses of the Middle East have not
made indigeneity and its implications central to understandings
of the politics and sociology of the Middle East. Instead, such
groups typically have been examined through the prism of security,
through the perspective of imperialist and colonial interests of, for
example, Britain, France or Russia, or through the security perspective of nation-states that have seen them as a threat throughout the
twentieth century. When indigenous groups have been discussed
through the perspective of human rights, on the other hand, they
have been conceptualised as minorities in their respective nation-
states, rather than as indigenous groups extending beyond state
boundaries, whose collective rights need international protection.
In terms of academic scholarship, conceptualisation of Kurds or of
other groups in the Middle East as indigenous is not non-existent. It
has been considered, yet such works are few and far between. More
importantly, even fewer think about diasporic indigeneity.

Yet Kurdish demands for autonomy, and for linguistic and cultural rights, are similar to the indigeneity claims pursued by indigenous groups in Latin America. Furthermore, there are some

examples of Kurds being conceived as an indigenous group in the media, by civil society organisations, in think-tank reports and in government reports. Kurds frame their demands by deploying themes of indigeneity, if not also through the language of indigeneity and coloniality. This is unsurprising given that, 'For most of the [Turkish] Republic's history, the southeast [Kurdish populated regions] has been ruled under martial law and emergency regulations' (Gambetti and Jongerden, 2015: 3). Yet much of the discussion on Kurds continues to frame them in the language of twentieth-century nation-states or the notion of statelessness. This locks them into a state-centric world-view and understanding rather than their claims being understood as an indigenous group spread over different nation-states, with alternative claims and conceptualisations of sovereignty and citizenship. The sovereignty claims of indigenous groups thus challenge the world order, which is predicated on the nation-state; they do not just concern the nation-states in which they live.

The discussion around indigenous rights is thus inextricably intertwined with the idea of sovereignty. Defenders argue that the international law and order as it stands has not distributed sovereignty in a just way. They thus position indigenous rights as correctives to the existing international order and law. Furthermore, the defenders of indigenous rights argue that vulnerable groups and cultures need special protection, as without this protection they will be crushed under the dominant-national culture. Protections brought by the UN Declaration on the Rights of Indigenous Peoples (UNDRIP) (United Nations, 2007) are thus a 'third-generation' right, after 'individual rights' brought by the Universal Declaration of Human Rights (United Nations, 1948) and the international covenants on economic and social rights (1976) and on civil and civic rights (1976, 1989). The UNDRIP declaration is not legally binding, but it is an important document that delineates various individual and collective rights. It has come about through the Indigenous Peoples Movement campaigning over many years through an international order (and its mechanisms), which itself constituted the nation-state as the primary sovereign actor of international order.

Two central issues have helped, and will continue to pave the way for a further rethinking of Kurds as an indigenous group. One is due to Rojava, the other is due to the Kurdish diaspora. The fight against ISIS in Rojava has allowed Kurds to nurture their connections and links across different countries in the Middle East and to further conceive of themselves as an indigenous resistance against invasion. It has empowered this sentiment for Kurds and sustains it, despite their losses, failures and current precarious situation. The emotional ties and identity connections created by Rojava are significant for identity, memory and belonging. Second, it is the Kurdish diaspora that has enabled themes of indigeneity in relation to Kurds to be further nurtured and sustained and to have become transnational. Even though diasporic Kurds have had to establish their economic security and stability after their arrival in Europe and beyond, many have either remained political or, through meeting other Kurds, became political and more assertive over time in diaspora. This was echoed to me in interviews – for example, 'I became a Kurd in London; I became a Kurd thanks to imperialists.' Living in subaltern neighbourhoods of Western cities, and armed with solidarity and support from other subaltern groups and discourses, and left-wing organisations, the diaspora activism helped to conceive Kurds as peoples under colonial occupation – they secured this not just among Kurds but also transnationally and among non-Kurds. Cultural expressions of Kurdish indigeneity, such as traditional dancing (*govend*), music, the Newroz story and celebrations in Europe, pastoral themes such as mountains, rivers and shepherding, and political mobilisations bring Kurds from disparate parts of Europe together. They firm up connections from different regions with each other and the diaspora to the homeland. Cultural expressions of indigeneity also bond different generations of Kurds. This is not to say that indigeneity themes and discourses were not already deployed in the past. A Kurdish MP from the pro-Kurdish party HDP Gülten Kışanak, while speaking in the Turkish parliament in 2012, said, 'We have been in these lands for centuries … We are here. We have been, for long histories.'[11] Connections with the land and peoples were often made even if these did not always go hand in hand with the modernisation ideology that dominated the earlier phases of the Kurdish movement.

In conclusion, diasporic activism has increased indigeneity themes and claims by Kurds, and made their indigeneity transnational. It enabled Kurds to be conceived as 'indigenous people under colonial occupation', even if the word 'indigeneity' itself is not always adopted by Kurds themselves. The Kurdish diaspora, through Rojava and notwithstanding existing homeland activism, has enabled themes of indigeneity in relation to Kurds to be further nurtured and sustained and to become transnational. This indigenous drift is not always easily identifiable in discourse. Nor are Kurds explicitly accommodated under the existing legal framework of the UNDRIP. Yet indigeneity delineates a particular type of consciousness and existential mindset, and epistemological questioning of colonial knowledges. Even if associated rights are not present, indigeneity themes and discourses foster a particular type of Kurdish identity, and as such they will probably continue to weave Kurdish identity not just spatially but also temporally.

This chapter has provided detailed understanding of the Kurdish diaspora and its trajectory by employing themes of diaspora as translation and decoloniality. After a discussion of the Kurdish presence in Europe, both numerically and in terms of activism, I examined how the Kurdish diaspora carry out different types of ethno-political translations of their struggle in Europe. I did this by examining their translations to two specific audiences: other diasporic Kurds in Europe and their fellow European citizens. I identified that the Kurdish struggle is translated to European audiences in an informative way, focusing on Kurdish suffering and deploying the language of human rights. To newer generations of Kurds, the translations of ethno-political identity and struggle employed an emotive language, focusing on dignity, rebellion and uprising, attempting to galvanise younger generations of Kurds in Europe. I discussed the importance of culture, music and dancing in translating Kurdishness, as well as how some translations went 'wrong' when European sensitivities were misunderstood, how other Kurds were at times 'misread', and when younger Kurds' commitment to the Kurdish struggle was over-estimated. I also looked at how three specific aspects of the Kurdish struggle were translated to both the newer generations of Kurds in Europe and to non-Kurds in Europe, examining the comparisons made between Mandela, the Irish and Kurds, the Rojava Revolution and the issue of female guerrillas. I discussed the various translation strategies that were employed, including rewriting, foreignising, domesticating, not understanding and compensating. An examination of the discourses of Kurds reveals how they rewrite Kurdish politics, undo colonisation and carry out both foreignisations and domestication in their engagements with the Global North, exposing links between their predicament, Europe and colonialism. Such translations of Kurdish identity and struggle are not only central for the transnational battles of Kurds, they also link up with attempts to decolonise dominant discourses about them. By making discussions of empires, indigeneity and transnationalism central to my discussion of Kurdish diaspora, I expanded the spatial and temporal dimensions of the research on Kurdish diaspora. I moved it away from methodologically nationalist approaches which have typically trapped examinations of Kurds and Kurdish diaspora within nation-centric and state-centric conceptualisations. The chapter also rethought Kurdish diaspora globally by conceiving Kurdish diaspora as transnational indigenous resistance. It is expected that in the years to come, the Kurdish diaspora in Europe and beyond will continue to play a significant role in reinforcing indigenous themes, if not claiming it as a stance. It is thus interesting to note that an indigenous identity is being anchored via the translations and decolonisations of the Kurdish diaspora – that is, by those who initially had to dis-anchor themselves from their homeland.

Notes

1 Unless qualified in another way, the word 'struggle' used throughout this book refers to the variety of efforts pursued by Kurds. It varies from resistance and rebellion to mobilisation and to simple demands of recognition of Kurdish language, culture and identity. The Kurdish struggle movement refers to the diverse variety of Kurdish groups, including insurgencies and actors, activists and legal political parties, that represent the Kurds.
2 Four countries recognise the Anfal campaign as a genocide (Norway, Sweden, South Korea and the United Kingdom).
3 For a discussion of the PKK's insurgency and how it unsuccessfully tried to transform itself and the conflict towards non-violence, as well as the emergence and development of the legal political parties that represent the Kurds, see Gunes (2012).
4 For various reports of this conflict and human rights abuses, see Human Rights Watch (2010, 2012).

5 According to the report of the United Nations High Commission for Human Rights (2017), since the collapse of the ceasefire with the PKK in 2015, hundreds have been killed during operations against the PKK, and many alleged unlawful and civilian killings remain un-investigated. Crackdowns on Kurdish political leaders have escalated since 2015. The co-chairs of the pro-Kurdish party Peoples' Democratic Party (HDP), Selahattin Demirtaş and Figen Yüksekdağ, remain imprisoned on terrorism charges since 2016 (despite the European Court of Human Rights ruling for Demirtaş's immediate release in 2020). Pressures on the media have also intensified. Many Kurdish mayors and town councillors have been removed through an emergency law, and replaced with central appointees. According to Zeid Ra'ad al-Hussein, the United Nations High Commissioner for Human Rights, the state of emergency in Turkey 'target[s] criticism, not terrorism'. Turkey has continued to launch military attacks against Kurdish militants and positions in neighbouring Iraq and Syria.

6 Country name or national identity were changed respectively.

7 The word 'Kurdistan' indicates the region that is populated by Kurds. Even though its use is still highly controversial in Turkey, during the Ottoman empire there was a sizeable province under this name, Eyalet-i Kurdistan. It was the successor to the Diyarbakır province. According to Özok-Gündoğan (2020: 983), 'Both before the establishment of and after the liquidation of the "Kurdistan Eyaleti-province", Ottoman authorities used the term "Kurdistan" liberally and openly to refer to the eastern provinces, which had been historically under the command of the Kurdish nobility.'

8 *Serhildan* means rebellion in Kurdish – it especially refers to the Kurdish uprisings and protests that have been taking place since the 1990s. Previous significant Kurdish rebellions include the Sheik Said rebellion in 1925 in Diyarbakır; the Ağrı Rebellion of 1927–30 and the Dersim uprising of 1937.

9 H&M, a high street clothing company, developed a range of clothing based on Kurdish female fighters' uniforms (see Gupta, 2016).

10 *Marie Claire*, a fashionable woman's magazine, published an article by Griffin (2014) on the Women's Protection Unit (YPJ) under the title 'These Remarkable Women are Fighting ISIS: It's Time You Know Who They Are'.

11 Kışanak was accused of making speeches that supported the PKK. She was arrested in 2016 and in 2019 was jailed for 14 years. She was previously imprisoned in 1980 during the military coup.

5

Backlash to diaspora in the Global North

Imperialistic abroad and xenophobic at home.

(Venuti, 1995: 23)

This book has so far focused on the translations and decolonisations in which diasporas engage. It ventured outside the two common theorisations of diaspora and instead employed some of the insights of translation studies in order to enrich our understanding and conceptualisation of diaspora. I expanded diaspora from being merely trapped in discussions of nation-states, and in particular limited to a conceptualisation that sees diaspora limited to 'ethno-political' struggles and violence within nation-states, and consequent push factors. This is because many of today's diasporas, like nation-states, are an outcome of historic relationships arising out of subordination and colonisation, of expansion and retraction of populations associated with empires. I placed translation and decolonisation at the centre of diasporic subjectivity, experience, engagement and mobilisation. I also defended the argument that our conceptualisations of diaspora should make central the ways in which diasporas translate identity, how they foreignise and how they have been, and continue to remain as, a corrective to colonialism. Diaspora needs to be understood in relation to colonialism, imperialism and history. It is linked to the movements of peoples from former colonies – be they the Caribbean, Vietnam, Ghana, Algeria or places where there are continuing forms of exclusion, violence and oppression that are structured and embedded further through global exclusions. I provided examples of diasporas in the Global North, but also discussed a case study of this by examining the Kurdish diaspora in Europe, and by linking diaspora to an understanding of the global social order via notions such as transnational indigeneity and Global South. My aim in this chapter is to push further with this need to position diaspora at the centre of our understanding of contemporary global social order, especially in the age of the rise of nativism, exclusive nationalism and White identity politics.

Immigration is seen as engulfing the world – not just the Global North but also the Global South. However, this is not a crisis of migration, but rather a socio-political crisis. The immigration issue is closely tied up with a sense of loss of control and a deep sense of anxiety about being invaded and overrun by peoples from elsewhere. It is not surprising that concerns about migration are evident in the language and discourses of European nativists (e.g. Marie Le Pen in France, Geert Wilders' Party for Freedom in the Netherlands, Matteo Salvini's far-right Lega Party in Italy, Viktor Orbán of Hungary, the Spanish Vox Party in Spain, the Swedish Democrats, Alternative for Germany, the Freedom Party of Austria, Greece's Golden Dawn, the Danish People's Party, UKIP in the United Kingdom and the Swiss People's Party). They were central to the success of the campaigns of Brexit and Trump, Modi and Bolsonaro. The political crisis about migration continues to affect mainstream parties around the world, with nativists able to take them over and push for more hostile migration regimes.

However, it would be a mistake to narrowly conceive the rise of nativism as being a response to new arrivals or to the 'crisis' about new migrations. As I will show in this chapter, the rise of such sentiments is in fact closely linked to resentments towards settled diasporas and against measures that have challenged exclusive nationalism. In the Global North, anxieties about new migrations are deeply intertwined with existing diasporas of colour – be they the Roma in Eastern Europe, Arabs in France, Africans in Italy, Mexicans in the United States or South Asians in the United Kingdom. It would also be wrong to conceive of White nativism as a far-right or a right-wing issue, as it has gained traction with certain sections of the left (Bloomfield, 2020; Mondon and Winter, 2019; Shilliam, 2020). This backlash to diaspora in the Global North is a central concern of this chapter. Below, I will seek to examine the 'backlash to diaspora' by taking the UK example and by looking at two discourses, 'anti-multiculturalism' and the notion of 'the left-behind'/'traditional' working class. My aim is not to defend or rehearse arguments about multiculturalism, or the politics of the working class *per se*. I will instead discuss how two specific discourses have gained ascendancy, increasingly employed in the service of exclusive nationalism and together both undermining the equality and dignity claims of diasporas and underhandedly valorising Whiteness. I am especially interested in unpacking why and how they have had such purchase, the contexts in which they arose and what they reveal about the normative and social order in which we live.

Anti-multiculturalism as an exclusivist national identity

In the age of nativist ascendancy in the Global North, it has become commonplace to approach immigrants as a problem, if not to see them as a threat with which one needs to deal. The 'threat' of immigration, of being swamped, of losing control and the discomfort of having to deal with one's country's diminished role in the world, as well as alienation, all play a major role in many nativist campaigns. However, nativism cannot be fully made sense of without understanding loss of privilege *vis-à-vis* existing visible diasporas in the Global North. As I will discuss below, such campaigns and 'revolts' are also a reaction to a perceived loss of a Western way of life. They are to do with loss of sovereignty at home, namely a resistance to racial equality and to the existing racial/colonial social order being challenged through multiculturalist discourses and racial equality. In fact, anti-immigration sentiments are closely bound up with, if not at times used as a proxy for, showing discomfort about existing visible diasporic communities. In the United Kingdom, for example, the Brexit campaigns did not just criticise the European Union, but were also critical of the liberal and inclusive attitudes and policies that had developed in the previous 40 years – for example, multiculturalism, cosmopolitanism, diversity and inclusion. It is no coincidence that, among the Leavers' list of dislikes and what they saw as a social ill, multiculturalism was at the top, even over and above immigration – even if only slightly (Demir, 2017c).

Empirical research identified 'feeling that "the American way of life is threatened" is a consistent predictor of Trump support' (Mutz, 2018). A similar trend has been recognised by Sobolewska and Ford (2019: 148), who identified examining the British Election Study of 2016, that 'those who felt strongly that equal opportunities had gone too far and saw immigration as a threat to British culture, voted Leave by an overwhelming 85–15 margin'. Following the Black Lives Matter protests in the summer of 2020, the UK government turbo-charged its resistance to 'loss of sovereignty at home' – for example, by criticising the teaching of critical race theory and White privilege, reacting to the National Trust's 2020 report which showed connections between National Trust properties, colonialism and historic slavery (Huxtable et al., 2020). In September 2020, the culture secretary Oliver Dowden sent a ministerial edict to museums and funding bodies (Dowden, 2020), and followed this up in 2021 with a warning to charities and heritage institutions not to 'do Britain down'. The UK government also announced that it would appoint a 'free speech champion' for English universities, implying that free speech was curbed in favour of inclusivist agendas while at the same time attempting to intervene and regulate history, culture and education. Such attempts stoked culture wars for electoral support, but also undermined years of gradual progress on multiculturalism, equality and diversity across universities and schools, and the heritage and museum sector in the United Kingdom. They actively worked to reproduce an exclusivist national identity.

Anti-multiculturalism is at first sight a paradox. Social science research shows that there is increased social contact between different ethnic groups, including increased inter-ethnic marriage (Muttarak and Heath, 2010). 'Mixed' ethnicity is one of the fastest growing ethnic groups in the United Kingdom (Finney and Simpson, 2009: 99). Residential segregation has decreased (Catney, 2013) and claims that ethno-religious groups lead parallel lives (e.g. Cantle, 2001, 2015) have been found to frequently be overstated empirically and exaggerated (Amin, 2002; Finney and Simpson, 2009). Research instead signals that, despite problems, 'all [minority] groups alike have displayed major change across the generations in the direction of a British identity and reduced social distance' (Heath and Demireva, 2014: 161). There has also been a general shift in that societies are becoming more tolerant and social distance between groups is decreasing (Ford, 2008; Storm, Sobolewska and Ford, 2017). However, multiculturalism in this period came to be derided for harming social cohesion and solidarity. This anti-multiculturalism is worth reflecting upon.

Anti-multiculturalism is different from criticisms of multiculturalism. I associate anti-multiculturalism with subversion and follow the distinction made by Asad (1995: 328): 'Whereas critique has pretensions to shared standards of reasoning and justice, subversion assumes a state of war and a determination to eliminate the enemy.' Anti-multiculturalism is an attempt to re-establish hegemonic racial and ethnic sovereignty – in this case, Whiteness – against the remedial policies of inclusion. I thus see it as attempting to undermine the gains made towards equality and accommodations achieved over the years through the struggles and mobilisations of diasporas. It harks back to the assimilationist strategy of the pre-1970s, which sought assimilation into structures of hierarchy and segregation. Anti-multiculturalist discourses also use explanations based on ethnicity, culture and difference to explain the isolation and segregation of 'others', instead of paying attention to how racialised and other structural inequalities intersect and create exclusions. They focus the gaze on minorities. Anti-multiculturalist discourses rely on essentialist understandings of culture (and of religion), deeming groups and cultures hermetically sealed. Structural explanations used for explaining why poor White communities are isolated are not offered to communities of colour. Instead, such discourses and policies place the burden of responsibility on the shoulders of Britain's ethnic minority populations while at the same time fighting against policies that are meant to alleviate racial inequality and include them. As a discourse, the power of anti-multiculturalism lies in its ability to discredit racialised non-hegemonic others without mentioning race, and to dignify exclusive nationalism without mentioning the nation.

In public, policy and media discourse, the dislike of multiculturalism often emerges within nationalist and conservative responses – for example, among media figures (e.g. Peter Hitchens) and politicians (e.g. David Cameron). Multiculturalism is disdained not just because it is tied to an increased racial and religious diversity on its own. I argue that multiculturalism is disliked primarily because visible diasporas no longer 'know their place'. Minorities are seen as having gone too far in their aims to question the supremacy of the hegemonic nationals and demands for equality. In this sense, anti-multiculturalism is closer to the anti-feminist discourses that accuse women of having gone too far, and of asking for too much equality. Anti-multiculturalism does not necessarily signal a longing for homogeneity, just as anti-feminism is rarely about not having women out and about. It is more about maintaining the racial and cultural status quo and hierarchy, reinforcing the idea that the nation belongs to some more than others. I see anti-multiculturalism as being uncomfortable with interventions that seek to remove existing inequalities of power, and the weaponisation of arguments on freedom against minorities, through the deployment of discursive strategies such as 'PC culture', 'woke' and 'cancel culture' (Titley, 2020). Nor do we often hear anti-multiculturalist discourses deployed against, for example, Americans or Australians in Europe, or the French living in London, or the English living in Germany. Instead, a close focus is maintained on diasporas of colour, especially if the accommodations they seek are underpinned by cultural and religious difference or racial equality. In other words, gains in terms of increased inclusion of previously othered and colonised peoples into the polity have come under attack not just from people who perhaps never liked the arrival and presence of visible diasporas in the first place, but especially by those who resist becoming equals. For such an equality threatens how hegemonic nationals have typically and historically been regarded as the archetypal citizens. Anti-multiculturalism is thus one of the convenient ways of defending exclusive national identity.

Attacks on multiculturalism have not always come from the right, either. There are plenty who deem themselves to be situated on the left who have been critical of it (e.g. Kenan Malik, Hugo Young, David Blunkett, Paul Scheffer, Ted Cantle). Multiculturalism is seen as instrumentalist and as part of a liberal agenda. It is seen as 'identity politics' and posited against class politics, with the latter seen as the true path to salvation. A close focus on racial and cultural exclusions is posited as a distraction, and against what is perceived as the more urgent problem of class exclusions. The often-quoted Twitter feed of Ta-Nehisi Coates, an African-American author, has replied to this ridicule: 'Notion that White dude's issues are "economic" and everybody else is just trying to discuss their feelings is, well, sorta deplorable' (Twitter, 1 December 2016). A worry is also often expressed in terms of multiculturalism blocking the possibility to criticise 'other' cultures, despite leading multiculturalist theorists making dialogue and criticism across and within communities a central part of this philosophy (Parekh, 2000; Taylor, 1992). Critics often ignore that multiculturalism is closely linked to the anti-racist struggle and history. Nor do they acknowledge that class is also an identity, and by seeking to focus exclusively on class, they fail to see how other divisions – for example, race and gender – intersect with class visions. More importantly, they ignore that capitalism is racialised (Roediger, 2007; Virdee, 2014). Not to reproduce racist (or sexist) tropes and stereotypes is problematised as a type of muzzling. In so doing, the proponents of this perspective at times end up doing the job of nativists in their resistance to, and at times mockery of, multiculturalism. They make it difficult to increase the claim-making capacities of the minoritised towards equality, even if those who are racially minoritised are a large part of the working class whose rights they seek to defend. It is indeed wrong to conceive of anti-multiculturalism as a problem that emanates purely from the right.

Anti-multiculturalism has also found various articulations in political and policy debates, usually allied with concerns about 'sleepwalking into segregation', as expressed by Ted Cantle's report from 2001 following the Bradford Riots, and later by then Prime Minister David Cameron's anti-multiculturalism rhetoric. Such sentiments have often been repeated by Trevor Philips (2016), the former chairman of the Equality and Human Rights Commission (EHRC). They were reproduced in the 2016 Casey Review. David Goodhart, a vocal anti-multiculturalist who was appointed in November 2020 as an EHRC Board member, has positioned solidarity against diversity (Goodhart, 2004, 2017). In this juxtaposition, the connection between the imperial past and diverse today, and hence the historic links and claims of diasporas of colour upon the nation, are denied. Diversity is seen as an impediment to national solidarity. Racialised melancholia (Gilroy, 2004) and racialised amnesia are able to feed off and reproduce one another. Anti-multiculturalism, different from mere criticisms of multiculturalism or varieties of it, incites the idea that national majorities continue to hold the upper hand. The discourses of 'self-segregating communities', 'parallel lives', 'sleepwalking into segregation' and other allied claims have in fact led us to 'sleepwalk into myth-making'; as

Finney and Simpson (2009) show in their detailed analysis, many of these claims are found to be problematic and exaggerated.

Multiculturalism, however, has not only been attacked in wider media and popular and political discourses; it has also been criticised in academia – this time posited against cosmopolitanism. For example:

> Multiculturalism means plural monoculturalism. It refers to collective categories of difference and has a tendency to essentialize them ... multiculturalism perceives cultural differences as – so to speak – 'little nations' in one nation.
>
> (Beck, 2011: 54)

> Cosmopolitanism is not a generalised version of multiculturalism where plurality is simply the goal.
>
> (Delanty, 2006: 35)

> Multiculturalism, too, often results in an increase in cultural differences as opposed to being a means to secure autonomy and justice.
>
> (Delanty, 2011: 650)

> Ours is an effort to move beyond multiculturalism, and to go beyond the ultimately essentializing nature of culturally and ethno-religious-based paradigms.
>
> (Glick Schiller, Darieva and Gruner-Domic, 2011: 401)

The attack on multiculturalism in academia occurred around the same time as right-wing leaders in Europe – Cameron, Merkel and Sarkozy – started their chorus of public criticism and attacks on multiculturalism, most famously in their Munich Security Conference speeches in 2011. Such simplistic accounts of multiculturalism are difficult to follow, if not rather uncomfortable, when in fact non-hierarchical acceptance of and engagement with others is central to cosmopolitanism, and also essential to the different varieties of multiculturalism. The opposite of multiculturalism is monoculturalism, and assimilation or segregation; it is not cosmopolitanism. Such swift dismissal of multiculturalism, like the caricatured versions offered by Cantle (2001, 2015), fails to effectively recognise multiculturalism's historical struggles against the assimilationist and segregationist policies of the old order, including its history of anti-racism. When accompanied by problematic understandings of Europe and modernity (Bhambra, 2014,

2017), and a lack of understanding of diversity being constitutive of the European past, they become all the more problematic. They reinforce otherness through signalling a story of Europe where others are always seen as 'coming in' and 'being tolerated' while Europe and Europeans are presented as engaged in unencumbered cosmopolitan ventures (Demir, 2016). Another reason for the opposition to multiculturalism seen among social theorists such as Beck (2011) arises from their allegiance to the classic binary between tradition and modernity, and their building up of a vision of modernity that posits the unencumbered reflexive modern self against group rights, multiculturalism and religion. For them, group rights and religion remain in the domain of particularism, essentialism and tradition, and have the potential to curb (or even subvert) the modern self and its existing relationship with the secular nation-state and/or the transnational/cosmopolitan order. Essentialist ways of understanding culture and religion, and multiculturalism, pervade their social theories.

What is interesting is that around the time when such discourses, from some sections of the left and the right, were deployed in pursuit of anti-multiculturalism, the 2011 UK census showed that over that decade residential segregation had 'decreased within most local authority districts of England and Wales, for all ethnic minority groups' (Catney, 2013: 1). The last phrase, 'for all ethnic minority groups', is important. This is because the group that saw the largest increases in segregation comprised the White British and other White groups – although the increase was marginal (Catney, 2013: 4). Using data from the 2011 census, Catney (2013: 2) provides examples of cities such as Leicester and Birmingham, which had seen a decrease in segregation by 5 per cent since 2000. She identifies that, 'Manchester experienced a decrease in segregation for all ethnic groups, including by 13 per cent for the Indian ethnic group. Segregation has decreased in Bradford for all ethnic groups, except a marginal (under 2 per cent) increase for the White British and Other White groups' (Catney, 2013: 2). In other words, the argument about 'sleepwalking into segregation' was deployed to criticise ethnic minorities and multiculturalism who 'kept to themselves' at a time when residential segregation in the United Kingdom had decreased for all groups – except for Whites where there was an increase (albeit small).

Anti-multiculturalists, including those on the left, also overlook the phenomenon of White flight – that some White residents who can afford it leave areas if they become 'too diverse'. For example, according to the 2011 Census, between 2001 and 2011 the percentage of Whites in Leicester fell from 60.5 per cent to 45.1 per cent; Birmingham followed suit, with the percentage of Whites falling from 65.6 per cent to 53.1 per cent. However, this did not necessarily happen because White people in these cities moved from areas which were poor and ghettoised, with poor housing or high crime rates. For example, in Leicester the ward of Evington is an area that has good housing and higher than average economic activity levels for Leicester – yet this area is increasingly being deserted by Whites (Open Society Institute, 2010). In the national imaginary, monocultural suburbs, if populated by Whites, are deemed 'normal', whereas diverse and multicultural inner-city areas are seen as 'segregated'.

During the very same time that the United Kingdom saw an increase in the anti-multiculturalism discourse, there was also evidence of other forms of integration, as illustrated through the educational success of many ethnic minority groups in the United Kingdom. In the very period when 'multiculturalism' and integration were problematised, many groups of pupils – especially those from African, South Asian and East Asian backgrounds – 'have either pulled further away from White British pupils or have caught up with them, to some degree' (Hutchinson et al., 2019: 13). The success and integration of children from these backgrounds, despite being economically left behind overall, have not always been welcomed as a sign of integration in Britain. Instead of such examples being seen as further evidence of integration, the increasing educational success of ethnic minority students is used to inflame the crisis about Whiteness and victimhood. Referring to Nick Timothy's treatment of this issue Holmwood (2020) argues that, 'Rather it [their success] is taken as an indication – with no evidence provided – that ethnic minorities have been unfairly supported.' This is unsurprising, given how the claim that their 'ethnic minority rights and culture' were posited against 'our ordinary' people by the Red Tories as well as Blue Labour (Shilliam, 2018, 2020), as nostalgia for past glories, faith, flag and family became their catch-cry (Bloomfield, 2020). Evidence of integration is also illustrated in other research – for example, Asian Muslim pupils in Burnley 'were found to be more tolerant than their White peers especially those in all-White schools', and they were more likely to be interested in learning about religions other than their own compared with White pupils. In Oldham, 'the social networks of minorities were found to be more diverse than Whites' (Finney and Simpson, 2009: 104).

A return to a discussion of exclusive national identity around Whiteness is thus required. Multiculturalism is at times deployed to mean 'diverse', that is to express an empirical fact. For example, Leicester is referred to as a multicultural city when what is meant is diverse. Others use it to refer to the instrumentalism associated with diversity management, corporate multiculturalism and city council multiculturalism and thus tokenistic. Multiculturalism as a normative position is, of course, much more than these. It is not merely about celebrating diversity or difference; its history is long and is tied to the anti-racist struggle by postcolonial 'immigrants'. It is part and parcel of their struggle against exclusionary and assimilationist policies of the 1950s and 1960s. It is a struggle for inclusion against aggressive majoritarianism, and involves many varieties and revelations (e.g. Hall, 2000). Multiculturalism, however, is not divorced from racial diversity. For we know that those who are uncomfortable with racial diversity 'tend also to reject targeted policies designed to offer redress for racial disadvantage' (Sobolewska and Ford, 2019: 150).

Multiculturalism as a normative argument is closely related to particular demands such as protection from racism, rejection of assimilation, allowing minorities to make claims on national identity and not just on themselves, and making accommodations to include others who would otherwise be excluded (Modood, 2007). Like other political theories, there are varieties of multiculturalism – for example, conservative, liberal, deconstructive and radical. Multiculturalism has developed as a challenge to an exclusive nationalist identity (Demir, 2016, 2017c) on two counts. The first is the rejection of the assimilationist policies of the old order: multiculturalism and its associated policies aim to question the upper hand that the hegemonic national/racial/ethnic subjects hold, addressing inherited power relations and de-stabilising the dominance of the dominant identity. The second is the demand for the participation of minoritised groups on an equal footing as civic and political citizens: multiculturalism seeks to move minoritised groups from being seen as subjects of assimilation and domination to actors who can make transformative claims not just about themselves but also on the whole of the national and civic identity.

Multiculturalism seeks to dethrone the idea of national homogeneity and attempts to equalise power relations and increase the claim-making capacities of minoritised groups. It is part of the 'democratic settlement relating to diversity' that attempted to overturn the assimilationist and segregationist trends before it. North American multiculturalism has also been a vehicle for defending the rights and claims of, for example, LGBTQ+ communities, the disabled and women as minoritised groups. Adjustments are made to include all in the polity, correcting long-established processes of disadvantage. Yet there are many ways of and strategies for doing this, ranging from conservative multiculturalism to critical multiculturalism to unsettled multiculturalism (Hall, 2000; Hesse, 2000). There are also differences in approaches of countries towards migration, citizenship and multiculturalism (e.g. Favell, 1998). Multiculturalism thus has a number of varieties and can be critically engaged. Yet difference and diversity should matter, especially when they are linked to power. Multiculturalist demands require a loss of privilege, cultural power and sovereignty for the dominant racial and cultural group within a nation. Once this is recognised, we get closer to why anti-multiculturalism has been simmering and festering since the 1990s.

This antagonism to migration and diversity, and a distaste for liberal-left values, came to be justified and rationalised – for example by Goodhart (2004, 2017) – on the basis that they disrupt the cohesion of the (White) majority, in effect arguing that the equality demands of ethnic minority communities are divisive and corrosive. Far from being an enemy of cohesion and solidarity, as Goodhart has claimed, multiculturalism could instead be viewed as a vehicle for achieving cohesion and solidarity. Kaufmann's (2018) focus has also been on White cultural traditions and the assimilation of minorities to those traditions. Kaufmann identifies multiculturalism as central to explaining the current nativist movements. Yet, like Goodhart, he finds the White backlash to be justified. Arguing that racial self-interest of majorities is legitimate, he defends assimilation in order to calm down Whites who are concerned about losing power numerically and culturally. In such understandings, 'multicultural' comes to be associated with 'loss' and 'threat', and diasporas of colour as destabilising and divisive, blamed for disrupting the nation's cohesion and the solidarities therein. Patrimony, solidarity and belonging are not expanded to ethnic others; they continue to remain as 'other', reproducing essentialist understandings of culture and of ethnicity. Majority grievances are seen as legitimate, and consequently exclusivist ethnic and cultural identity is defended (Goodhart, quoted in Policy Exchange, 2017; Kaufmann, 2018).

Anti-multiculturalism is, of course, also a useful discursive strategy. It allows people to oppose 'their multiculturalism' without immediately exposing their own nativist and ethnocentric world-views. There are interesting similarities here to the way in which the notion of 'West' was adopted to bypass direct discussions of Whiteness in the late nineteenth and twentieth centuries. Bonnett (2008) discussed how it became possible to observe that explicit affirmations of White supremacism had begun to wither away only to be replaced by 'the West' and 'Western'. The latter helped to bypass racial connotations, but still allowed supremacy to be rightfully claimed. I argue that anti-multiculturalism has come to serve a similar purpose since the turn of the millennium. We should take anti-multiculturalism seriously, as it has become a convenient shortcut, a trope for defending exclusive national identity. In the twenty-first century, the equality demands of diasporic communities could be denied, solidarities around hegemonic identity (Whiteness) could be defended and majority grievances could be justified through discourses of anti-multiculturalism.

In order to understand the backlash to diaspora in the Global North in the twenty-first century, we also need to understand how anti-multiculturalism has become a code word for problematising Muslim populations in the West. It has come to channel Islamophobia. The attack has been twofold – first in the form of pathologising and demonising the lifestyles of Muslims, and second in the form of the introduction of a security agenda, hostile policing and other mechanisms of social control to monitor Muslims. It has occurred through scapegoating of Muslims, problematising Muslim women's dress, the Prevent agenda and also through increased measures that keep a close tab on Muslim schools (Holmwood and

O'Toole, 2017). Muslims continue to be stigmatised and to attract more hostility than other groups in the Global North. According to Storm, Sobolewska and Ford (2017: 410), Muslim Britons 'are singled out for negative attention from many British residents of all other backgrounds, including a large number who do not express hostility to other groups'. This is also widespread in other parts of the Global North. As Göle argues (2017: xvii), Muslims have become 'an overriding symbol of difference against which national identities are dressed and political agendas are set in the Western world'. They are also made to account for who they are, and to justify their beliefs and whether they can be trusted for inclusion into the polity as equals. It is thus highly interesting how multi-culturalism – a standard liberal ideology that demands dialogical engagement (e.g. Taylor, 1992 and Parekh, 2000) – has come to be deployed by anti-multiculturalists as a foil for defending major-itarianism. Anti-multiculturalism, and specifically Islamophobic stances, are revealing in terms of how some are refused entry to the polity as legitimate and equal members.

Anti-multiculturalism in the twenty-first century is thus highly important and relevant for understanding the backlash to diaspora in the Global North. However, much of the analysis on the rise of nativism and populism has tended to focus on anti-migrant sen-timent or socio-economic issues. While these are important, they are not sufficient. Multiculturalism was simply part of the demo-cratic liberal settlement that saw the ills and wrongs of the assimi-lationist ideology and segregationist policies. It is connected to the adjustments required for equal and fair participation and rose in opposition to assimilation of the racial colonial order. If we are to understand the global political order and the rise of nativism, we need to understand and consider the backlash to existing diasporas of colour being expressed in the form of anti-multiculturalism rather than focusing just on anti-immigrant feelings. Anxiety about loss of control at the borders is inextricably intertwined with loss of privilege and control *vis-à-vis* existing diasporas of colour in the Global North.

The discourse of a 'left-behind'/'traditional' working class as an exclusivist national identity

Alongside anti-multiculturalism, the discourse of 'the left-behind', used as a code word for the White working class, has become central to setting political agendas. 'The left-behind' is also used interchangeably with phrases such as 'traditional' working class and 'ordinary' working class, the latter also popularised by former British Prime Minister Theresa May. Such discourses tap into the existing worry and 'crisis about Whiteness'. This 'crisis' is not new: its antecedents exist, as I discuss below. In the twenty-first century, it has yet again been revived, crescendoed in the anxieties around Whites becoming 'hostages in their own country', and is increasingly being deployed in wider social and political debates in the media and academia. For example, Hochschild (2016) and Gest (2016) have turned their attention to Whites who have been left behind, discussing the alienation and disenfranchisement felt by those in blue-collar jobs. It has had other intellectual enablers, such as David Goodhart (2017), Eric Kaufmann (2017, 2018), Eatwell and Goodwin (2018), and Goodwin and Kaufmann (2020). These works identify anxieties about loss of privilege, power and demographic dominance as important drivers of excessive nationalism and defensive White identity politics. The problem is that they find such anxieties to be justified and legitimate. Their discourse has centred on White voters deserving special policy intervention. Kaufmann (2017, 2018) and Goodhart (Policy Exchange 2017) have openly defended White identity politics as a legitimate grievance, arguing that 'White self-interest is not racism'.

There is a growing body of scholarly research and analysis that examines the anxieties of White majorities since 2010 by critically engaging with the idea of 'the left-behind'/'traditional' working class *vis-à-vis* the recent rise of nativism in the United Kingdom and the United States (e.g. Bhambra, 2017; Crampton, 2016; Demir, 2017c; Dorling and Tomlinson, 2019; Holmwood, 2020; Inglehart and Norris, 2016; Mondon and Winter, 2019, 2020; Roediger, 2017; Sayer, 2017; Shilliam, 2020; Tilley, 2017; Virdee and McGeever, 2018). Empirical research (e.g. Mutz, 2018; Norris and Inglehart, 2019) has challenged that populist and nativist support can be explained by a change in wellbeing, resentment of economic inequality or social deprivation. Jardina (2019: 9) has argued that the rise of 'white identity politics is not wholly or even primarily rooted in economic disenfranchisement'. The research of Antonucci et al. (2017) contests the dominant view that Leave voters during Brexit were left behind economically. The research findings show that the Leave vote is not associated with 'working-class identification' but with 'middle-class' and 'no class' identification. Rae (2016) and Jump and Michell (2020: 1) show that there is no correlation between voting for Leave and living in a deprived area 'once higher educational attainment or occupational composition are controlled for the association becomes negative'. In the United States, the epitomisation of the Trump vote as revolt of 'the left-behind' was just as problematic (Henley, 2016). The 2016 and 2020 US elections show that Trump's support base was wealthier than that of his rivals in both the 2016 and 2020 elections. While only 42 per cent of those who earned $50,000 or less voted for Trump, 54 per cent of those who earned $100,000 or more voted for him (*New York Times*, 2020). In 2016, 'working-class whites voted far more like whites as a whole than like Black and Latino working-class voters. Indeed, racial identity (along with regular church attendance and being a veteran) far better predicted a Trump vote than income level did' (Roediger, 2017).

Data and research thus do not support the mainstream argument that nativist movements are the revolt of 'the left-behind'/'traditional' working class. Such discourses take no notice of the non-White poor and working classes that have been left behind for decades, discounting them from accounts of the nation. Interestingly however, the public, media and academic attention continues to focus on the 'left-behind'/'traditional' working class. I argue that its salience and popularity continue as the power of 'the left-behind'/'traditional' working class discourse lies in its ability not just to mobilise and re-energise anxieties about the decline of Whiteness, but also in its ability to conflate hegemonic ethnic and racial identity (Whiteness in the Global North) with national identity, to depict the former as the nation and thus to reinforce the idea that some belong more than others.

Anxieties about White degradation are not new (e.g. Bonnett, 2008; Du Bois, 1998 [1935]; Roediger, 2007, 2017; Tilley, 2017; Virdee, 2014). Working-class formation and the development of Whiteness have reinforced each other in the United States, but also in the way the nation is narrated in the United Kingdom. In the

United States, Du Bois (1998 [1935]: 237) has traced how the relative condition of the White worker has been an ongoing concern since the emancipation of slaves, arguing that the refusal to 'recognize black labour as equal and human' had undermined working-class unity and solidarity. Roediger has examined how much of workers' rights were won in the United States in an effort to keep the relatively raised condition of the White worker *vis-à-vis* the Black worker and how 'the "white worker" developed as a self-conscious social category mainly by comparing himself to Blacks' (Roediger, 2007: 23). The idea that the civil rights movement was going too far and too quickly, and that it was alienating Whites, was dominant throughout the 1960s. As Jardina (2019: 139) notes, on 9 November 1963, not long after Martin Luther King Jr delivered his famous 'I have a dream' speech, Pulitzer-winning *New York Times* columnist Russell Baker wrote about Whites no longer being listened to and losing their first-class status: 'His basic complaint is that he has become a second-class citizen and finds it harder and harder to keep his self-respect.' In the 1960s in the United States, when desegregation was being rolled out and racial hierarchies were being questioned, Republican votes in poor White neighbourhoods increased through fears of White decline. Associated feelings of White grievance did not wither away after the civil rights movement in the United States. In the 1990s, for example, research identified that many Whites in the United States felt that they faced significant discriminations and that their group was not getting the opportunities it deserved (Gallagher, 1997). Other research in this period also identified that for many Whites there existed racial prejudice and perceived competition from minorities, as well as a sense of entitlement that they should have more – even when they were socially, politically and economically in a more advantaged position (Bobo and Hutchings, 1996). More recent research shows that Whites with higher racial consciousness, not necessarily Whites who were poor or economically left behind, adopted White racial solidarity and White identity politics in the United States (Jardina, 2019). Discourses of 'What about poor White people?' (Allen, 2009) signal the ongoing historical racial alliance between Whites rather than a concern with poverty or class.

Seeing Whites constituting a justified aggrieved group is neither novel nor specific to the United States, of course. Similar concerns have also existed in the United Kingdom. Bonnett (1998) has examined the racialisation of White poor people as Whites, and traced how the working class came to be seen as White in Britain. Such racialisations and 'anxieties over perceived economic and cultural diminution of status – that is, being "left behind" had already accompanied discussions in the late 1960s over Commonwealth immigrations' (Shilliam, 2018: 156) and also during the arrival of African Asians to the United Kingdom in the 1970s. In the United Kingdom, Powell's 'Rivers of blood' speech was concerned with Commonwealth citizens. It sought to remove the right of settlement of Commonwealth citizens in the United Kingdom, demanding their re-emigration. What needs to be remembered is that in that speech, Powell also attacked the anti-discrimination legislation. It was delivered when the British Parliament was in fact considering the Race Relations Bill. Powell received much support and popularity across the country, including from trade unions. While anti-racist solidarities between the working classes of all colours existed, such remedial laws were often seen by some Whites as a setback to their own wellbeing, and led to mobilisations around Whiteness, albeit couched in the language of class. The negative reaction to anti-racism and multicultural policies in education and equal provision of local services (e.g. housing) existed throughout the 1990s in the United Kingdom. Solomos and Back (1996) and Virdee (2014) have recorded how tensions were created between anti-racist and multiculturalist policies on the one hand, and working-class politics on the other, and at times explicitly between White and non-White workers. Just as demands for more equality, desegregation and civil rights multiplied the discourses of 'White neglect' in the United States (along with votes for the Republicans), the same trend occurred in the United Kingdom, with the Conservatives gaining footholds in many working-class areas. Following Brexit, such a trend could again be seen clearly in the United Kingdom – Conservatives were able to gain the votes of White working class areas, especially in the North of England, and were able to crack Labour's 'Red Wall' – for example, in Hartlepool in 2021 – partly by appealing to nativist sentiments and discourses of 'White neglect'.

The relationship of race and class is also essential to understanding the establishment of the welfare state in the West. The welfare state needs to be understood in relation to the decolonisation of peoples elsewhere and the granting of new advantages to White workers in the United Kingdom. As has been identified, 'working-class white identity was bound up with a sense of racial owner-ship of an emergent "welfare-state"' (Bonnett, 2005: 10), despite being significantly funded through extraction and revenues from the colonies (Bhambra, forthcoming). The recent expressed sym-pathies with the blue-collar workers epitomised as a 'left-behind revolt' should also be considered as part and parcel of a crisis that includes the neoliberal restructuring of the welfare state, austerity and the worsening of rights and privileges provided by the welfare state, pitting deprived White and non-White groups against one another. As Bonnett (2005) and Inwood (2019) argue, the 'crisis of Whiteness' has been shown to emerge at times of crisis, when privileges are disrupted or challenged; I turn to this shortly.

This perceived crisis is sustained by an undercurrent of victimhood and an allied environment of moral panic, as identified by research:

> Evidence points overwhelmingly to perceived status threat among high-status groups as the key motivation underlying Trump support. White Americans' declining numerical dominance in the United States together with the rising status of African Americans and American insecurity about whether the United States is still the dominant global economic superpower combined to prompt a classic defensive reac-tion among members of dominant groups. (Mutz, 2018)

In this climate, the notion of 'the left-behind'/'traditional' working class (Shilliam, 2020) received much purchase and became a code word for the 'forgotten White Americans' or for those 'embattled British people in their own island'. Such tropes fuelled the senti-ment that they were faring worse than they deserved and that others (diasporas of colour) had got ahead because they were getting special treatment. Such loss and deprivation are felt especially deeply by those who are tied to the idea that the nation belongs to some more than others. 'The left-behind' discourse used as a proxy for the White working class engages racially conservative voters and their feelings of loss of privilege, and is used to justify 'the idea that the (White) working class is to be prioritised against the arrival of undeserving (multi-ethnic) newcomers scrounging on Britain's hard-achieved prosperity' (Snoussi and Mompelat, 2019: 9). Overall, such expressions of victimhood reveal the taken-for-granted assumption that Whites are the natural and ordinary citizens, and that they should be prioritised in educational, health and welfare provision despite being 'factually better off than their non-White ethnic minority neighbours who continue to experience an "ethnic penalty" in income, employment and health experiences' (Miah, Sanderson and Thomas, 2020: 207).

In such times, while hegemonic nationals are presented as marginalised, the disadvantages minorities highlight on race and othering are written off. The diasporic 'other' is blamed for disrupting the nation's cohesion. A crisis of Whiteness, together with ideas about White decline, steer towards a defensive (and popular) mobilisation of the legitimate (White) members of the nation, instead of identifying the structural inequalities that prevent the working class of all colours from gaining power, resources and opportunities. The introduction of the discourse of 'the left-behind'/'traditional' working class and the accompanying nativist narrative must thus be understood as a story and discourse fuelled by an interplay of anxieties of Whiteness and exclusionary nationalism. It redeems the hegemonic racial and ethnic identity as the national identity, deserving special attention and help at the expense of others.

As I explained above, similar 'vulnerabilities of Whiteness' have emerged in the past, especially when Whites perceive their privileges to be threatened: 'the perceived threat to Whiteness historically has led to a wave of White supremacist violence' (Inwood, 2019: 586). However, we should remember that 'vulnerabilities of Whiteness' also emerged when Whiteness was in its ascendancy, confirming its success in being able to provide a backdrop for all occasions:

> Although more and more of the world was passing into white control, by the last years of the nineteenth century, there had emerged a ready market for those who were feeling fretful about the quality of military recruits, the poisonous influence of city life, the rise of feminism, the spectre of intra-European rivalries, the falling birth rate of the middle classes and many other things beside. These manifold worries were grouped together as a white racial crisis. Whiteness was

opened out and made an object of middle- and upper-class 'worry' by these discourses.

(Bonnett, 2005: 11)

This 'left-behind'/'traditional' working-class argument has had much purchase, as it was able to signal race without mentioning race, by not problematising the ethnic others directly, but rather via invoking tradition, nostalgia, good old times, and old-fashioned Britishness. 'The left-behind' was thus a convenient way for 'fighting for a way of life', yet through being couched as a fight for the economically disadvantaged. In our 'post-racial times', it fostered a sense of victimhood without always needing to mention Whiteness or racialised others. There is much research which shows that women, ethnic minorities and migrants typically have been erased from dominant British working-class narratives of the nation (e.g. Danewid, 2017; Virdee, 2014). Virdee (2014) has identified how central the othering of those who were Irish Catholic, Asian, Jewish, African and Caribbean was to British class formation. In a similar vein, 'This [left-behind] narrative and the identification of whiteness with the working class, negates its privilege and renders it the "people"' (Mondon and Winter, 2019: 512). The deployment of 'the left-behind'/'traditional' working class label does not just erase the racial and ethnic diversity of the working class, its history and today; the narrative created around it also has the potential to curtail and harm class struggle itself. I discuss this next.

Such appeals to the White working class have recharged White identity politics. Appeals to White labour and 'offering them alliance' were, and continue to be, a significant aspect of the reconstruction politics in the United States following the emancipation of slaves (Du Bois, 1998 [1935]: 633). Du Bois (1998 [1935]: 708) warned us that we should not expect 'this social upheaval [ending of slavery] was going to be accomplished with peace, honesty and efficiency, and that the planters were going quietly to surrender the right to live on the labour of black folk after two hundred and fifty years of habitual exploitation'. This recent emergence is thus part of the 'the long history of white resentment and fear' over losing continuing privileges and demographic decline (Inwood, 2019: 593). White identity politics relieves the worries and anxieties of the White population; it tells them that their concerns are being listened to and acted upon. It allows White alliances across the social divide. It conceives 'posh' Whites and poor Whites as coming together through Whiteness, taking control and fighting against being 'swamped in our own country'. The privilege and class elitism of those who lead nativist movements can be resolved through White solidarity. It clearly undermines class struggle, as it conflates the interests of the economically and politically powerful with those of the (White) poor. 'The left-behind' has a 'wide appeal across classes because its core message is of racial rather than class solidarity' (Sayer, 2017: 102). Such White identity politics 'presents White people's actions in defence of their existing advantages (and their continued oppression of others) as a "legitimate" form of identity politics' (Gillborn, 2019: 99). It has often been employed as a counter-revolutionary tactic to divide the working class and resist structural changes during times of capitalist economic crisis (Gilmore, 1999). It seems that what happened after the 2008 financial crisis did not disappoint in this regard, reigniting White identity politics.

White identity politics 'writes out' the racialised outsiders – that is, diasporas of colour and new migrants, who now constitute a large section of the working class – from the narrative of the working class. Recent research on the working class in the United Kingdom narrates the lived experiences of both non-White and White working class, and identifies a significant overlap between them: 'rather than the 'white working class' and 'ethnic or migrant working class' living different or separate lives, we found significant overlap in everyday lived experiences' (Snoussi and Mompelat, 2019: 3). It is curious that White identity politics has risen at a time when relative differences between poor Whites and poor racialised others have decreased. It is perhaps that this race card is all the more valuable in such times, when privilege is questioned and is on the wane. This has been identified as 'White hegemonic alliance', namely the 'tacit race-based agreement' between poor and non-poor Whites, central to ensuring that their respective economic and social benefits are secured (Allen, 2009: 211). White identity politics, at least in the current climate, has proven to be rewarding for those who employ it, given that 'the sustained shift towards more diverse societies and more positive views of diversity is seen as threatening by the declining but still substantial segment of the white electorate that holds racially conservative views' (Sobolewska and Ford,

2019: 149). It is sustained by a curious mixture of British exceptionalism, racial superiority and declinism – the so-called collapse of White prestige. It usefully taps into the discourse of 'taking back control', not just by establishing strong borders, but by also taking back control from diasporas of colour *within* who 'no longer know their place'. White identity politics and culture wars will probably continue to be politically useful mobilisation strategies in the forthcoming years, recruiting those both from the political right and the left, increasing racial rather than class solidarity.

The discourse of 'the left-behind'/'traditional' working class has had a wide reception and purchase, as it is rather disarming. It complements the anti-austerity stance of those on the left, and it is seen to be attending to the interests and concerns of the working class and the poor. It is a powerful code word for signalling those who are forgotten. It invokes authenticity, a concern for the poor; it connotes vulnerability. Yet there is little evidence of a concern for working class and poor people of all colours among those who valorise 'the left-behind'/'traditional' working class. Working-class people do not fare well economically or educationally, but there is no additional disadvantage and discrimination that the working class people who are White face due to being White in addition to that faced by ethnic minorities who are working class: 'Whiteness in and of itself is not a barrier to social and economic success and anti-whiteness is not a widespread violent racist ideology' (Tilley, 2017).

Indeed, there is little attention paid to class, and much paid to Whiteness in discourses of 'the left-behind/'traditional'. Many ethnic minority communities are economically left behind. They experience worse labour market conditions, are poorer overall and were hit much harder by austerity (Bassel and Emejulu, 2018). In fact, ethnic minorities were left behind for decades, with a history of higher rates of unemployment than Whites, often paying an ethnic penalty – a disadvantage that cannot be accounted for by other reasons such as education. According to Bell and Casebourne's (2008: 3) report, which looks at this longitudinally, 'Ethnic minorities continue to experience higher unemployment rates, greater concentrations in routine and semi-routine work and lower earnings than do members of the comparison group of British and other Whites.' This is also ascertained by other research: 'White ethnic groups (with the marked exception of the Gypsy or Irish Traveller group) [are] in a more advantaged position in the labour market compared with other ethnic groups' (Nazroo and Kapadia, 2013).

In the United Kingdom, some ethnic minorities have responded positively to education and have made substantial gains. However, despite their increasing educational success and attainment levels, they continue to lose out in the job market and in terms of pay and career progression. Ethnic minorities with degrees in high-status professional careers pay an 'ethnic' penalty, even when other factors are controlled for (Friedman and Laurison, 2019). Other research identified a substantial ethnic pay penalty (17 per cent) for Black male university graduates in the United Kingdom (Henehan and Rose, 2018). The barriers to employment and social mobility remain persistent. Yet the notion of the 'left-behind' is not afforded to them. Ethnic minorities are typically written out of 'the left-behind' discussions as they do not fit the racialised connotations constructed around 'the left-behind'/'traditional' working class. Additionally, those it leaves out are well aware of this fact. Research shows that such concepts are often tied to an entitlement about Whiteness and privilege, which is well-known by ethnic minorities themselves: 'The racialisation of "working class" to mean "White British" was clearly identified as a source of alienation for BME people specifically' (Snoussi and Mompelat, 2019: 38). The discourse of 'the left-behind'/'traditional' working class (and, at times, 'ordinary' working class) has become a useful strategy for racial messaging via class. It has become a convenient code that disarms while proving to be an armoury for excessive and exclusive (White) nationalism.

In conclusion, nativism is not only a reaction to economic or political globalisation, or to new migrations, but also to increased racial, cultural and religious diversity and multiculturalism at home. Both are to do with loss of sovereignty. The first is tied to the loss of power, economic prowess and sovereignty of their country in the world, demonstrated as a reaction to globalisation, interdependence and longing for Empire 2.0, coupled with a belief in own innate superiority. Nativist discourses are peppered with a longing for the good old times when they held the upper hand in world politics, when they were a great 'trading nation' or when they were great or coming first – for example about 'Putting the "Great" Back into Great Britain' (UKIP, 2017), 'America First', 'Make the Netherlands

Great Again' (Wilder's slogan) and 'Austria First' (the campaign message of Hofer's Freedom Party). The second loss of sovereignty is the loss of power of the hegemonic White nationals over others *within* the nation. In this chapter, I have focused on this latter loss, and argued that the backlash to diasporas of colour in this century in the Global North can be identified via exclusive nationalisms and the deployment of two specific discourses: of anti-multiculturalism and of 'the left-behind'/'traditional' working class.

These two discourses, particularly together, are central to understanding the resentments of nativism and the rise of White identity politics in the twenty-first century in Britain and beyond. The power of 'the left-behind'/'traditional' working class discourse lies in its capacity to valorise Whiteness without mentioning race; and the power of anti-multicultural discourse lies in its ability to discredit equality demands through a critical gaze and scrutiny of cultural others. A particular White identity politics is carried out by concealing overly race-based talk through culture (anti-multiculturalism) and class ('the left-behind'/'traditional' working class). The chapter has not wished to explain away concerns about class or culture by calling them misplaced; instead, it has sought to show what particular dominant discourses on culture and class reveal about the anxieties of our times, especially who is included into, and excluded from, the accounts of the nation.

I examined how anti-multiculturalism relies on and reproduces essentialist understandings of culture, and how the discourse of 'the left behind'/'traditional' working class, through valorising Whiteness, in fact hampers class solidarity and struggle. It ignores the racial diversity of the working class and erases the non-White poor and working-classes who are ethnic minorities from national accounts (Anderson, 2013). Together, these discourses reject diasporas of colour as legitimate and equal members of the nation while in the same breath accusing them of failing to integrate. I argued that such discourses reproduce ideas about how some belong to Britain (or the West) more than others; how some should be prioritised in public provision; how some are seen as the natural and ordinary citizens, while others are underhandedly refused as legitimate and equal members of the nation – even if many ethnic minorities and migrants fare worse on many indicators, and even when they occupy key worker roles, disproportionately losing their lives working in a pandemic and serving the nation (Bhambra, 2017, 2020).

The chapter discussed how such discourses have emanated from those on both the left and the right. It also discussed how anti-multiculturalism arose when residential segregation was decreasing, social distance between groups was identified as reduced and attachment of minorities towards a British identity had increased (Heath and Demireva, 2014: 161); the discourse of 'the left-behind'/ 'traditional' working class emerged as the British working class increasingly comprises migrants and people of colour. Concerns about White neglect will probably continue, if not strengthen, if White privilege is seen as deserving and entitled, yet on the wane. Given this backlash to diaspora, this far-reaching rise of White identity politics and the increased stoking of culture wars for elect-oral gain in Britain since the Black Lives Matter protests in 2020, we must now pause, ask and consider: who has really been playing the race card here?

Conclusion

In this book, I have explored the insights and limitations of diaspora theorising and attempted to move it forward through a focus on how diasporas do translation and decolonisation, offering conceptual tools such as 'diaspora as rewriting and transformation', 'diaspora as erasure and exclusion' and 'diaspora as a tension between foreignisation and domestication'. I provided examples and also applied such concepts to the study of Kurdish diaspora, demonstrating their heuristic potential. In the final chapter, the book also considered 'the backlash to diaspora' in the Global North, this time paying attention to how discourses of anti-multiculturalism (over and above criticisms of multiculturalism) and 'the left-behind'/'traditional' working class have become codes for valorising exclusive (White) nationalisms. Reinforcing one another, these discourses crescendoed as part of a backlash to the equality demands of diasporas of colour in the twenty-first century, as I showed in the example of the United Kingdom. These discourses conveniently write out and exclude diasporas of colour and their struggles for equality from the narrative of working class solidarity and that of the nation while simultaneously pointing the finger at them for failing to integrate.

In this concluding chapter, I will summarise the kind of understanding that diaspora translation and decolonisation can bring by thinking about the propositions of the book through the prism of time and space. In her seminal *Cartographies of Diaspora: Contesting Identities*, Brah (1996) introduces her concept of diaspora space:

> Diaspora space as a conceptual category is 'inhabited' not only by those who have migrated and their descendants but equally by those who are constructed and represented as indigenous. In other words, the concept of diaspora space (as opposed to that of diaspora)

includes the entanglement of genealogies of dispersion with those of
'staying put'.

(Brah, 1996: 181)

Brah was able to stretch our understanding and imagination on
diaspora over and beyond those who move. Can we further expand
diaspora space, and also diaspora time, by making translation and
decolonisation central to our analysis of diaspora?

Safran's (1991: 83) forceful and pertinent claim from the 1990s
that ethnicity and migration have paid 'little if any attention ...
to diasporas' came to be challenged about fifteen years later by
Brubaker who explored the 'explosion of interest' in diaspora
within that period, and claimed that the term had proliferated and
was put into the service of various 'intellectual, cultural and political
agendas' (2005: 1). What had happened in those fifteen years? In
that period, two central approaches to diaspora theorising emerged,
one focused on the key characteristics of diaspora, often with an
emphasis on origins, roots and soil. These works examined 'diaspora as a being'. The second approach came to conceive of diaspora
differently. 'Diaspora as a becoming' paid considerable attention
to subjectivity, fluidity and hybridity when discussing diaspora.
Scholars from this tradition were successful in employing diaspora
in order to challenge essentialist understandings of race and ethnicity through an examination of diasporic subjectivity. This, however, led to understandings of diaspora as revolving around fluidity,
mobility and transnational flows, and to some extent has deprived
research from acknowledging, identifying and unpacking the transformative and radical potential of diaspora.

This book has sought to change the terms of the discussion
of diaspora, which have orbited around these two dominant
formations. Instead, it has suggested that we, as analysts, focus
on how diasporas do translation and decolonisation, and offered
conceptualisations that include, among other things, 'radical
remembering', 'radical inclusion', 'diaspora as rewriting and transformation', 'diaspora as erasure and exclusion' and 'diaspora as a
tension between foreignisation and domestication'. I attempted to
break free of discussions of diaspora, which too often examine it
within the confines of the nation-state. Methodologically nationalist approaches to diaspora that also ignore the role of empire
have brought both spatial and temporal limitations to diaspora

theorising. They have brought temporal limitations because, methodologically nationalist approaches have reduced diaspora analysis to push factors and ethno-political struggles *within* a nation-state. They have erased, or at best omitted, an examination of the links between empire and diaspora. Diaspora should instead be understood as inscribed and entangled in a series of historical and political processes associated with empire and expansion – including, of course, nationalist and ethno-political responses to these. Severing the links between diaspora and empire has meant that diaspora scholarship has not sufficiently examined how diasporas can become agents of decolonisation, and how they question unequal and hierarchical relationships entrenched in empire. Lifting this temporal and analytical limitation can free the reach of diaspora and challenge collective amnesia. It can enrich how we understand the role and place of diaspora today – that is they not only fight against their othering and discrimination, but also have effected, and continue to shape, ideas about freedom, equality and human dignity globally.

Methodologically nationalist approaches have also brought spatial limitations to diaspora, theorising it too tightly in the language and understandings of the nation-state. If diaspora is to be understood as a transnational intervention, it should analyse and identify the new spatial connections diasporas make, such as transnational indigeneity, cosmopolitan solidarity and conviviality, which go beyond individualised plurality. Without the shackles of methodological nationalism, diaspora research can also allow us to desegregate different diasporic battles from one another, and register and explore diasporic solidarities. For example, it can push us to investigate the links between the mobilisations of Afro-Caribbean and South Asian diasporas or between Kurdish and Tamil diasporas, or between Rosa Parks in Montgomery, Alabama in the United States and the Bristol Bus Boycott in Bristol in the United Kingdom. It can open up comparative analysis, not just due to diaspora being a postcolonial phenomenon, but also because of the types of dislodging of coloniality it carries out. Diaspora research free of methodological nationalism also has the potential to enable us to reconcile colonial struggles with today's diasporic interventions – for example, the Black Lives Matter movement. Last but not least, the rejection of methodological nationalism can help to rebuff the assumption that the real home of diasporas remains elsewhere – that is, their nation-state – making their inclusion to the new home contingent and rescindable, even when there are extensive connections that were created through empire, as we saw in the Windrush Scandal.

Diaspora research that is underpinned by the insights of translation and decolonisation has the potential for us analysts to see and connect the struggles of diasporas in disparate locations, and also diasporas to their history and empire. We can therefore expand the space/time axes of diaspora research. Without reducing diaspora to a study of a racial or ethnic group, but not denying the centrality of race and ethnicity to diaspora, a focus on diaspora as translation and decolonisation can extend the use of diaspora both spatially and temporally, and allow us to see diasporas as mobilisations acting on and shaping globalisation. This provides room for an understanding of diasporic alliances and mobilisations across space, and diasporic roots in history and empire. It can therefore uncover the role of diaspora in global processes. Diaspora has always been inextricably connected to the global and the decolonial, so it is high time diaspora studies is too.

It is no coincidence that discussions of diaspora re-emerged and proliferated soon after the demise of Western/European empires, when some of the subjects of these empires moved to Western metropoles in the 1950s and 1960s and faced resistance. It is no coincidence that the concept took hold again when diasporas of colour started demanding adaptations and inclusions – although this time also respect and equality in the Global North in the 1980s and 1990s and were found to be 'rioting'. It should no longer be a surprise that 'diasporas of colour are back again', demanding decolonisation in the Global North, along with material, cultural and epistemological shifts, and responding to exclusive (White) national narratives and policies. A focus on translation and decolonisation provides diaspora research with a framework for linking such diasporic demands to what I identified as the backlash to diaspora in the Global North and diasporic communities' attempts to be included as legitimate citizens. The decolonising role of diasporas has, of course, not gone unremarked by diasporas and their offspring in the Global North. If anything, they were always there and are now resolutely back, as shown by movements such as Black Lives Matter.

This book has therefore sought to change the terms of the discussion of diaspora that have associated diaspora with in-betweenness, with diaspora often conceived of as a halfway house. Diasporas have long been portrayed as stuck between home and host, as peoples constantly straddling two cultures, falling through gaps, facing the 'the tyranny of in-betweenness'. At times, this gap is cherished as a way to show the depth and vigour of diaspora, involving naïve assumptions about authenticity and culture. In the field of diaspora studies, this gap is still often the underlying assumption and driver of theory, and perhaps even fetishised. Even the notion of hybridity typically conjures up bio-socially distinct entities coming together – although pureness has rightly been rejected by Gilroy (1993), for example. This book has resisted the reduction of diaspora to in-betweenness, to gaps or even to hybridity – no matter how cherished. Rather, armed with the insight from translation studies, it has discussed how diasporas understand, talk to and negotiate with, as well as unsettle, disrupt and decolonise, the new home and the home left behind. To study these, we need to uncover the ingenious ways in which diasporic actors translate, rewrite, represent, challenge and decolonise. In other words, we need to examine processes of translation and decolonisation rather than focusing on finished products of the home and of away. By examining the translational activities of the Kurdish diaspora, I aimed to provide a case study of the frictions as well as the lubricants of such translations and decolonisations, including exposing links between the Kurds' predicament, coloniality and the Global North.

Conceptualisations of diaspora underpinned by the 'straddling two cultures' view are also problematic in terms of us being able to understand, locate and respond to the backlash to diaspora that has soared since 2010. Such backlash has found its recent articulations in culture wars since the Black Lives Matter movement in 2020. In the summer of 2020, Ofcom received 24,000 complaints in the wake of a dance performance by Diversity on ITV's *Britain's Got Talent* TV show, which depicted the death of George Floyd with the central message of social cohesion and unity. Customers threatened to boycott Sainsbury's for its celebration of Black History Month, and later for featuring a Black family in its 2020 Christmas advertising campaign, accusing it of not showing any 'British' people in the advert. The National Trust was accused of adopting a 'woke' agenda and 'virtue signalling' after it published a report in September 2020 that examined the links between National Trust properties and slavery and colonialism. In September 2020 and again in early 2021, the culture secretary Oliver Dowden warned charities and heritage institutions, signalling a crackdown on them if they continued 'to do Britain down'. The backlash in the Global North has also attempted to silence academia, while ironically condemning 'cancel culture' and 'no platforming' at universities. For example, Donald Trump, Boris Johnson's government and some French academics have all made studies of critical race theory (CRT) a target alongside studies of White privilege and diversity training. These are calls for inconvenient truths to be ignored, omitted or screened off because they fundamentally conflict with the whitewashed image of the nation that they wish to portray. They seek to omit 'unsavoury' histories and facts while at the same time attacking 'cancel culture' and 'no platforming'. No irony is intended.

The backlash to diaspora and its recent revival in the form of 'culture wars' will probably remain a central axis of political debate over the next few decades, as they have proven to be politically productive and useful strategies for gaining votes and sustaining power in the Global North. In an increasingly globalised and interconnected world, the battle of diasporas will not go away any time soon. It is thus all the more important that we analysts continue to offer better conceptualisations of diaspora as diasporas translate, decolonise and thus shape the global world in which we live.

References

Africa Reparations Movement (UK) (1994) *Birmingham Declaration*, www.inosaar.llc.ed.ac.uk/sites/default/files/atoms/files/1994_bir-mingham_declaration.pdf(accessed 25 July 2021).

Ahmad, Aijaz (1992) *In Theory: Classes, Nations, Literatures*, New York: Verso.

Akala (2018) *Natives: Race and Class in the Ruins of Empire*, London: Two Roads.

Akbarzadeh, Sahram, Laoutides, Costas, Gourlay, William and Zahid, Shahab Ahmed (2020) 'The Iranian Kurds' Transnational Links: Impacts on Mobilization and Political Ambitions', *Ethnic and Racial Studies*, 43:12, 2275–94.

Alexander, Claire (2000) *The Asian Gang: Ethnicity, Identity, Masculinity*, Oxford: Berg.

Alexander, Claire (2018) 'Breaking Black: The Death of Ethnic and Racial Studies in Britain', *Ethnic and Racial Studies*, 41:6, 1034–54.

Alinia, Minoo, Wahlbeck, Östen, Eliassi, Barzoo and Khayati, Khalid (2014) 'The Kurdish Diaspora: Transnational Ties, Home, and Politics of Belonging', *Nordic Journal of Migration Research*, 4:2, 53–6.

Allen, Ricky Lee (2009) 'What About Poor White People?', in William Ayers, Therese Quinn and David Stovall (eds), *Handbook of Social Justice in Education*, New York: Routledge, pp. 209–30.

Allison, Christine F. (2016) 'The Shifting Borders of Conflict, Difference, and Oppression: Kurdish Folklore Revisited', in Gareth Stansfield and Mohammed Shareef (eds), *Kurdish Studies Revisited*, London: Hurst, pp. 115–33.

Am, Ash (2002) 'Ethnicity and the Multi-cultural City: Living with Diversity', *Environment and Planning*, 34, 959–80.

Anand, Dibyesh (2018) 'Diasporic Subjectivity as an Ethical Condition', in Klaus Stierstorfer and Janet Wilson (eds), *The Routledge Diaspora Studies Reader*, London: Routledge, pp. 114–19.

Anderson, Bridget (2013) *Us and Them: The Dangerous Politics of Immigration Control*, Oxford: Oxford University Press.

Anthias, Floya (1998) 'Evaluating "Diaspora": Beyond Ethnicity?', *Sociology*, 32:3, 557–80.

Anthias, Floya (2001) 'New Hybridities, Old Concepts: The Limits of "Culture"', *Ethnic and Racial Studies*, 24:4, 619–41.

Antonucci, Lorenza, Horvath, Laszlo, Kutiyski, Yordan and Krouwel, André (2017) 'The Malaise of the Squeezed Middle: Challenging the Narrative of the "Left Behind" Brexiter', *Competition and Change*, 21:3, 211–29.

Appadurai, Arjun (1991) 'Global Ethnoscapes: Notes and Queries for a Transnational Anthropology', in Richard G. Fox (ed.), *Recapturing Anthropology: Working in the Present*, Santa Fe, NM: School of American Research, pp. 191–210.

Arslan, Adem Y. (2005) 'Avrupa Kürtleri Kimlik Arayışında' (Europe's Kurds are in Search of Identity), *Aksiyon: Weekly News Magazine*, 20 December.

Asad, Talal (1986) 'The Concept of Cultural Translation in British Social Anthropology', in James Clifford and George E. Marcus (eds), *Writing Culture*, Berkeley, CA: University of California Press, pp. 140–64.

Asad, Talal (ed.) (1995) *Anthropology and the Colonial Encounter*, Lanham, MD: Humanities Press International.

Asad, Talal and Dixon, John (1985) 'Translating Europe's Others', in Francis Barker, Peter Hulme, Margaret Iversen and Diana Loxley (eds), *Europe and Its Others*, Colchester: University of Essex Press, pp. 170–7.

Ayata, Bilgin (2011) 'Kurdish Transnational Politics and Turkey's Changing Kurdish Policy: The Journey of Kurdish Broadcasting from Europe to Turkey', *Journal of Contemporary European Studies*, 19:4, 523–33.

Ayim, May (2003) *Blues in Black and White*, trans. Anne Adams, London: Africa World Press.

Back, Les and Sinha, Shamser (2016) 'Multicultural Conviviality in the Midst of Racism's Ruins', *Journal of Intercultural Studies*, 37:5, 517–32.

Bagguley, Paul and Hussain, Yasmin (2012) *Riotous Citizens: Ethnic Conflict in Multicultural Britain*, London: Routledge.

Bailey, Alison (2007) 'Strategic Ignorance', in Shannon Sullivan and Nancy Tuana (eds), *Race and Epistemologies of Ignorance*, New York: State University of New York Press, pp. 77–94.

Banerjee, Sukanya (2012) 'Introduction: Routing Diasporas', in Sukanya Banerjee, Aims McGuiness and Steven McKay (eds), *New Routes for Diaspora Studies*, Bloomington, IN: Indiana University Press, pp. 1–22.

Barnes, Barry, Bloor, David and Henry, John (1996) *Scientific Knowledge: A Sociological Analysis*, London: Athlone Press.

Bartram, David (2019) 'The UK Citizenship Process: Political Integration or Marginalization?', *Sociology*, 53:4, 671–88.

Başer, Bahar (2015) *Diasporas and Homeland Conflicts: A Comparative Perspective*, Aldershot: Ashgate.

Bassel, Leah and Emejulu, Akwugo (2018) *Minority Women and Austerity: Survival and Resistance in France and Britain*, Bristol: Policy Press.

Bassnett, Susan (1998a) 'The Translation Turn in Cultural Studies', in Susan Bassnett and André Lefevere (eds), *Constructing Cultures: Essays on Literary Translation*, Oxford: Marston Book Services, pp. 123–40.

Bassnett, Susan (1998b) 'When is a Translation Not a Translation?' in Susan Bassnett and André Lefevere (eds), *Constructing Cultures: Essays on Literary Translation*, Oxford: Marston Book Services, pp. 26–40.

Bassnett, Susan and Lefevere, André (1998) 'Introduction', in Susan Bassnett and André Lefevere (eds), *Constructing Cultures: Essays on Literary Translation*, Oxford: Marston Book Services, pp. 1–11.

Bassnett, Susan and Trivedi, Harish (1999) 'Introduction', in Susan Bassnett and Harish Trivedi (eds), *Post-Colonial Translation: Theory and Practice*, London: Routledge, pp. 1–18.

Bassnett-MacGuire, Susan (1991) *Translation Studies*, London: Routledge.

Bayır, Derya (2013) *Minorities and Nationalism in Turkish Law*, Farnham: Ashgate.

BBC (2011) 'Daily View: David Starkey's Comments on Race and Riots', www.bbc.co.uk/blogs/seealso/2011/08/daily_view_david_starkeys_comm.html(accessed 4 January 2021).

BBC (2012) 'Ugandan Asians Advert "Foolish", says Leicester Councillor' www.bbc.co.uk/news/uk-england-leicestershire-19165216 (accessed 4 January 2021).

BBC (2019) 'Who are the Kurds?', www.bbc.co.uk/news/world-middle-east-29702440(accessed 4 January 2021).

Beattie, John H.M. (1964) *Other Cultures*, London: Cohen and West.

Beattie, John H.M. (1970) 'On Understanding Ritual', in Bryan R. Wilson (ed.), *Rationality*, Oxford: Blackwell, pp. 240–68.

Beck, Ulrich (2011) 'Multiculturalism or Cosmopolitanism: How Can We Describe and Understand the Diversity of the World?', *Social Sciences in China*, 32:4, 52–8.

Bell, Laurie and Casebourne, Jo (2008) *Increasing Employment for Ethnic Minorities: A Summary of Research Findings*, London: Centre for Economic and Social Inclusion.

Benjamin, Walter (1968 [1923]) 'Task of Translator', in *Illuminations*, trans. Harry Zohn, ed. Hannah Arendt, New York: Harcourt Brace Jovanovich, pp. 69–82.

Benson, Susan (1996) 'Asians Have Culture, West Indians Have Problems', in Terence O. Ranger, Yunas Samad and Ossie Stuart (eds), *Culture, Identity and Politics*, Aldershot: Avebury, pp. 47–56.

Berman, Antoine (1992) *The Experience of the Foreign: Culture and Translation in Romantic Germany*, trans. Stefan Heyvaert, New York: State University of New York Press.

Berman, Antoine (2004 [1985]) 'Translations and the Trials of the Foreign', trans. Lawrence Venuti, in Lawrence Venuti (ed.), *The Translation Studies Reader*, London: Routledge, pp. 276–89.

Bhabha, Homi K. (1994) *The Location of Culture*, London: Routledge.

Bhambra, Gurminder K. (2007) *Rethinking Modernity: Postcolonialism and the Sociological Imagination*, Basingstoke: Palgrave Macmillan.

Bhambra, Gurminder K. (2014) *Connected Sociologies*, London: Bloomsbury.

Bhambra, Gurminder K. (2017) 'Brexit, Trump, and "Methodological Whiteness": On the Misrecognition of Race and Class', *The British Journal of Sociology*, 68:1, 214–32.

Bhambra, Gurminder K. (2020) 'Rethinking Brexit in the Light of COVID-19', Discover Society, https://discoversociety.org/2020/04/22/rethinking-brexit-in-the-light-of-covid-19 (accessed 4 January 2021).

Bhambra, Gurminder K. (forthcoming) 'Relations of Extraction, Relations of Redistribution: Empire, Nation, and the Construction of the British Welfare State', *British Journal of Sociology*.

Bhatt, Chetan (2000) 'Dharmo rakshati rakshitah: Hindutva Movements in the UK', *Ethnic and Racial Studies*, 23:3, 559–93.

Bielsa, Esperanca (2016) *Cosmopolitanism and Translation*, London: Routledge.

Bielsa, Esperanca and Bassnett, Susan (2009) *Translation in Global News*, London: Routledge.

Bilkhu, Raj Kaur (2019) 'Amritsar Massacre: Apology "Futile" Says Relative', BBC News, 13 April, www.bbc.co.uk/news/uk-england-coventry-warwickshire-47885148(accessed 4 January 2021).

Bloomfield, Jon (2020) 'Progressive Politics in a Changing World: Challenging the Fallacies of Blue Labour', *The Political Quarterly*, 91:1, 89–97.

Bloor, David (1997) *Wittgenstein, Rules and Institutions*, London: Routledge.

Bobo, Lawrence D. and Hutchings, Vincent, L. (1996) 'Perceptions of Racial Group Competition: Extending Blumer's Theory of Group Position to a Multiracial Social Context', *American Sociological Review*, 61:6, 951–72.

Bonnett, Alastair (1998) 'How the British Working Class Became White: The Symbolic (Re)Formation of Racialized Capitalism', *Journal of Historical Sociology*, 11:3, 316–40.

Bonnett, Alastair (2005) 'From the Crises of Whiteness to Western Supremacism', *Australian Critical Race and Whiteness Studies Association Journal*, 1:1, 8–20.

Bonnett, Alastair (2008) 'Whiteness and the West', in Claire Dwyer and Caroline Bressey (eds), *New Geographies of Race and Racism*, Aldershot: Ashgate, pp. 17–28.

Bourgois, Philippe (2003) *In Search of Respect: Selling Crack in El Barrio*, Cambridge: Cambridge University Press.

Boyarin, Daniel and Boyarin, Jonathan (2003) 'Diaspora: Generation and the Ground of Jewish Diaspora', in Jana Evans-Braziel and Anita Mannur (eds), *Theorizing Diaspora*, Oxford: Blackwell, pp. 85–118.

Bozarslan, Hamit (2001) 'Human Rights and the Kurdish Issue in Turkey', *Human Rights Review*, 3:1, 45–54.

Brah, Avtar (1996) *Cartographies of Diaspora: Contesting Identities*, London: Routledge.

Brah, Avtar (2018) 'Multiple Formations of Power: Articulations of Diaspora and Intersectionality', in Klaus Stierstorfer and Janet Wilson (eds), *The Routledge Diaspora Studies Reader*, London: Routledge, pp. 163–73.

Braziel, Jana Evans and Mannur, Anita (eds) (2003) *Theorizing Diaspora*, Oxford: Blackwell.

Brubaker, Rogers (2005) 'The "Diaspora" Diaspora', *Ethnic and Racial Studies*, 28:1, 1–19.

Bruinessen, Martin Van (1998) 'Shifting National and Ethnic Identities: The Kurds in Turkey and the European Diaspora', *Journal of Muslim Minority Affairs*, 18:1, 39–52.

Bruinessen, Martin Van (2013) 'Editorial', *Kurdish Studies*, 1:1, 1–3.

Callon, Michel (1984) 'Some Elements of a Sociology of Translation: Domestication of the Scallops and the Fishermen of St Brieuc Bay', *Sociological Review*, 32:1, 196–233.

Cantle, Ted (2001) *Community Cohesion: A Report of the Independent Review Team*, London: Home Office.

Cantle, Ted (2015) 'Interculturalism: "Learning to Live in Diversity"', *Ethnicities*, 16:3, 470–93.

Catney, Gemma (2013) 'Has Neighbourhood Ethnic Segregation Decreased?', *Manchester ESRC Centre on Dynamics of Ethnicity Bulletin*, http://hummedia.manchester.ac.uk/institutes/code/briefingsupdated/has-neighbourhood-ethnic-segregation-decreased.pdf(accessed 25 July 2021).

Cazeneuve, Jean (1972) *Lucien Lévy-Bruhl*, trans. Peter Riviere, Oxford: Blackwell.

Chariandy, David (2006) 'Postcolonial Diasporas', *Postcolonial Text*, 2:1, www.scribd.com/document/348611340/Postcolonial-Diasporas (accessed 4 January 2021).

Cheyfitz, Eric (1991) *The Poetics of Imperialism: Translation and Colonization from 'The Tempest' to 'Tarzan'*, New York: Oxford University Press.

Cho, Lily (2007) 'The Turn to Diaspora', *Topia: Canadian Journal of Cultural Studies*, 17, 11–30.

Clifford, James (1992) 'Travelling Cultures', in Lawrence Grossberg, Cary Nelson and Paula Treichler (eds), *Cultural Studies*, London: Routledge, pp. 96–116.

Clifford, James (1994) 'Diasporas', *Cultural Anthropology*, 9:3, 302–38.

Clifford, James (1997) *Routes: Travel and Translation in the Late Twentieth Century*, Cambridge, MA: Harvard University Press.

Cockburn, Cynthia (2017) *Looking to London: Stories of War, Escape and Asylum*, London: Pluto Press.

Cohen, Robin (1996) 'Diasporas and the Nation-State: From Victims to Challengers', *International Affairs*, 72:3, 507–20.

Cohen, Robin (1997) *Global Diasporas: An Introduction*, London: Routledge.

Cohen, Robin and Sheringham, Olivia (2016) *Encountering Difference*, Cambridge: Polity Press.

Cohen, Robin and Toninato, Paola (eds) (2010) *The Creolization Reader: Studies in Mixed Identities and Cultures,* London: Routledge.

Council of Europe (2006) The Cultural Situation of the Kurds, The Council of Europe Resolution 1519, https://assembly.coe.int/nw/xml/XRef/Xref-XML2HTML-en.asp?fileid=17477&lang=en (accessed 4 January 2021).

Crampton, Caroline (2016) 'Voting for Trump and Brexit: What the Working Class Revolt is Really About', New Statesman, www.newstatesman.com/world/north-america/2016/11/voting-trump-and-brexit-what-working-class-revolt-really-about(accessed 4 January 2021).

Cronin, Michael (1996) *Translating Ireland,* Cork: Cork University Press.

Cronin, Michael (2003) *Translation and Globalization,* London: Routledge.

Cronin, Michael (2006) *Translation and Identity,* London: Routledge.

Danewid, Ida (2017) 'White Innocence in the Black Mediterranean: Hospitality and the Erasure of History', *Third World Quarterly,* 38:7, 1674–89.

Delanty, Gerard (2006) 'The Cosmopolitan Imagination: Critical Cosmopolitanism and Social Theory', *British Journal of Sociology,* 57:1, 25–47.

Delanty, Gerard (2011) 'Cultural Diversity, Democracy and the Prospects of Cosmopolitanism: A Theory of Cultural Encounters', *British Journal of Sociology,* 62:4, 633–56.

Demir, Ipek (2012) 'Battling with Memleket in London: The Kurdish Diaspora's Engagement with Turkey', *Journal of Ethnic and Migration Studies,* 38:5, 815–31.

Demir, Ipek (2014) 'Humbling Turkishness: Undoing the Strategies of Exclusion and Inclusion of Turkish Modernity', *Journal of Historical Sociology,* 27:3, 381–401.

Demir, Ipek (2015) 'Battlespace Diaspora: How the Kurds of Turkey Revive, Construct and Translate the Kurdish Struggle in London', in Anastasia Christou and Elizabeth Mavroudi (eds), *Dismantling Diasporas Rethinking the Geographies of Diasporic Identity, Connection and Development,* London: Routledge, pp. 71–84.

Demir, Ipek (2016) 'Rethinking Cosmopolitanism, Multiculturalism and Diaspora via the Diasporic Cosmopolitanism of Europe's Kurds', in Gurminder K. Bhambra and John Narayan (eds), *European Cosmopolitanism: Colonial Histories and Postcolonial Societies,* London: Routledge, pp. 121–35.

Demir, Ipek (2017a) 'Shedding an Ethnic Identity in Diaspora: De-Turkification and the Transnational Discursive Struggles of the Kurdish Diaspora', *Critical Discourse Studies,* 14:3, 276–91.

Demir, Ipek (2017b) 'The Global South as Foreignization: The Case of the Kurdish Diaspora in Europe', *The Global South,* 11:2, 54–70.

Demir, Ipek (2017c) 'Brexit as a Backlash against "Loss of Privilege" and Multiculturalism', Discover Society, February, https://archive.discoversociety.org/2017/02/

01/brexit-as-a-backlash-against-loss-of-privilege-and-multiculturalism(accessed 4 January 2021).

Demir, Ipek (2021) 'Kurdish Transnational Indigeneity', in Hamit Bozarslan, Cengiz Gunes and Veli Yadirgi (eds), *Cambridge History of Kurds*, Cambridge: Cambridge University Press, pp. 829–47.

Demir, Ipek and Murtagh, Madeleine J. (2013) 'Data Sharing Across Biobanks: Epistemic Values, Data Mutability and Data Incommensurability', *New Genetics and Society*, 32:4, 350–65.

Derrida, Jacques (1979) 'Living on/Borderlines', trans. James Hulbert, in Harold Bloom (ed.), *Deconstruction and Criticism*, London: Routledge and Kegan Paul, pp. 75–176.

Dingwaney, Anuradha (1995) 'Introduction: Translating "Third World" Cultures', in Anuradha Dingwaney and Carol Maier (eds), *Between Languages and Cultures: Translation and Cross-cultural Texts*, Pittsburgh, PA: University of Pittsburgh Press, pp. 3–20.

Dorling, Danny and Tomlinson, Sally (2019) *Rule Britannia: Brexit and the End of Empire*, London: Biteback.

Douglass, Frederick (1999 [1871]) *Frederick Douglass: Selected Speeches and Writings*, ed. Philip Foner, Chicago, IL: Lawrence Hill Books.

Dowden, Oliver (2020) 'Letter from Culture Secretary to DCMS Arm's Length Bodies on Contested Heritage', www.gov.uk/government/publications/letter-from-culture-secretary-on-hm-government-position-on-contested-heritage (accessed 4 January 2021).

Du Bois, W.E. Burghardt (1998 [1935]) *Black Reconstruction in America 1860–1880*, New York: The Free Press.

Dwyer, Claire (2000) 'Negotiating Diasporic Identities: Young British South Asian Muslim Women', *Women's Studies International Forum*, 23:4, 475–86.

Eatwell, Roger and Goodwin, Matthew (2018) *National Populism: The Revolt Against Liberal Democracy*, London: Pelican.

Eccarius-Kelly, Vera (2002) 'Political Movements and Leverage Points: Kurdish Activism in the European Diaspora', *The Journal of Muslim Minority Affairs*, 22:1, 91–118.

Eddo-Lodge, Reni (2018) *Why I'm No Longer Talking to White People About Race*, London: Bloomsbury.

Eliassi, Barzoo (2013) *Contesting Kurdish Identities in Sweden: Quest for Belonging Among Middle Eastern Youth*, London: Palgrave Macmillan.

Ellison, Ralph (1995 [1964]) *Shadow and Act*, New York: Vintage.

Evans-Pritchard, Edward E. (1911) *Nuer Religion*, Oxford: Oxford University Press.

Evans-Pritchard, Edward E. (1981) *A History of Anthropological Thought*, ed. Andre Singer. London: Faber and Faber.

Fabian, Johannes (1986) *Language and Colonial Power: The Appropriation of Swahili in the Former Belgian Congo, 1880–1938*, Cambridge: Cambridge University Press.

Faist, Thomas (2010) 'Diaspora and Transnationalism: What Kind of Dance Partners?' in Rainer Bauböck and Thomas Faist (eds),

Diaspora and Transnationalism: Concepts, Theories and Methods, Amsterdam: Amsterdam University Press, pp. 9–34.

Favell, Adrian (1998) *Philosophies of Integration: Immigration and the Idea of Citizenship in France and Britain,* Basingstoke: Macmillan.

Favell, Adrian (forthcoming 2022) *The Integration Nation: Immigration and Colonial Power in Liberal Democracies,* Cambridge: Polity Press.

Favretti, Rema, Sandri, Giorgio and Scazzieri, Roberto (eds) (1999) *Incommensurability and Translation,* Cheltenham: Edward Elgar.

Finney, Nissa and Simpson, Ludi (2009) *Sleepwalking to Segregation? Challenging Myths About Race and Migration,* Bristol: Policy Press.

Foran, Lisa (2011) 'Translation as a Path to the Other: Derrida and Ricouer' in Lisa Foran (ed.), *Translation and Philosophy,* Bern: Peter Lang, pp. 75–88.

Ford, Robert (2008) 'Is Racial Prejudice Declining in Britain?', *British Journal of Sociology,* 59:4, 610–36.

Fortier, Anne-Marie (2017) 'The Psychic Life of Policy: Desire, Anxiety and "Citizenisation" in Britain', *Critical Social Policy,* 37:1, 3–21.

Fowler, Corinne (2020) *Green Unpleasant Land: Creative Responses to Britain's Colonial Countryside,* Leeds: Peepal Tree.

Fowler, Edward (1992) 'Rendering Words, Traversing Cultures: On the Art and Politics of Translating Modern Japanese Fiction', *Journal of Japanese Studies,* 18:1, 1–44.

Frazer, James G. (1980) *The Golden Bough: A Study in Magic and Religion,* London: Macmillan.

Friedman, Sam and Laurison, Daniel (2019) *The Class Ceiling: Why it Pays to be Privileged,* Bristol: Policy Press.

Friel, Brian (1981) *Translations.* London: Faber & Faber.

Fryer, Peter (1984) *Staying Power: The History of Black People in Britain,* London: Pluto Press.

Gallagher, Charles (1997) 'White Racial Formation: Into the Twenty-First Century', in Richard Delgado and Jean Stefancic (eds), *Critical White Studies: Looking behind the Mirror,* Philadelphia, PA: Temple University Press, pp. 6–11.

Gambetti, Zeynep and Jongerden, Joost (eds) (2015) 'Introduction: The Kurdish Issue in Turkey from a Spatial Perspective', in *The Kurdish Issue in Turkey: A Spatial Perspective,* London: Routledge, pp. 1–24.

Gentzler, Edwin (2001) *Contemporary Translation Theories,* Bristol: Multilingual Matters.

Gentzler, Edwin (2008) *Translation and Identity in the Americas: New Directions in Translation Theory,* London: Routledge.

Gest, Justin (2016) *The New Minority: White Working Class Politics in An Age of Immigration and Inequality,* New York: Oxford University Press.

Gilbert, Jeremie and Keane, David (2016) 'How French Law Makes Minorities Invisible', The Conversation, 13 November, https://theconversation.com/how-french-law-makes-minorities-invisible-66723(accessed 4 January 2021).

Gillborn, David (2019) 'We Need to Talk About White People', *Multicultural Perspectives*, 21:2, 97–101.

Gilmore, Ruth W. (1999) 'Globalization and US Prison Growth: From Military Keynesianism to Post-Keynesian Militarism', *Race and Class*, 40:2, 171–88.

Gilroy, Paul (1987) *'There Ain't No Black in the Union Jack': The Cultural Politics of Race and Nation*, London: Hutchinson.

Gilroy, Paul (1993) *The Black Atlantic: Modernity and Double Consciousness*, London: Verso.

Gilroy, Paul (1997) 'Diasporas and the Detours of Identity', in Kath Woodward (ed.), *Identity and Difference*, London: Sage, pp. 301–43.

Gilroy, Paul (2004) *After Empire: Melancholia or Convivial Culture?*, Abingdon: Routledge.

Glick Schiller, Nina (2014) 'Diasporic Cosmopolitanism: Migrants, Sociabilities and City-Making' in Nina Glick Schiller and Andrew Irving (eds), *Whose Cosmopolitanism? Critical Perspectives, Relationalities and Discontents*, New York: Berghahn, pp. 103–20.

Glick Schiller, Nina, Darieva, Tsypylma and Gruner-Domic, Sandra (2011) 'Defining Cosmopolitan Sociability in a Transnational Age: An Introduction', *Ethnic and Racial Studies*, 34:3, 399–418.

Gocek, Fatma Muge (2014) *Denial of Violence: Ottoman Past, Turkish Present, and Collective Violence Against the Armenians, 1789–2009*, Oxford: Oxford University Press.

Göle, Nilüfer (2017) *Daily Lives of Muslims: Islam and Public Confrontation in Contemporary Europe*, London: Zed Books.

Goodhart, David (2004) 'Too Diverse?', Prospect Magazine, www.prospectmagazine.co.uk/magazine/too-diverse-david-goodhart-multiculturalism-britain-immigration-globalisation (accessed 4 January 2021).

Goodhart, David (2017) *The Road to Somewhere: The New Tribes Shaping British Politics*, Harmondsworth: Penguin.

Goodwin, Matthew and Kaufman, Eric (2020) 'Where the Left Goes Wrong on National Populism: A Reply to Jon Bloomfield', *The Political Quarterly*, 91:1, 98–101.

Gopal, Priyamvada (2012) 'The Limits of Hybridity: Language and Innovation in Anglophone Postcolonial Poetry', in Joe Bray, Alison Gibbons and Brian McHale (eds), *The Routledge Companion to Experimental Literature*, London: Routledge, pp. 182–97.

Gopal, Priyamvada (2016) 'Redressing Anti-imperial Amnesia', *Race and Class*, 57:3, 18–30.

Gopal, Priyamvada (2019) *Insurgent Empire: Anticolonial Resistance and British Dissent*, London: Verso.

Griffin, Elizabeth (2014) 'These Remarkable Women are Fighting ISIS: It's Time You Know Who They Are', Marie Claire, 1 October, www.marieclaire.com/culture/news/a6643/these-are-the-women-battling-isis(accessed 4 January 2021).

Griffiths, David J. (2000) 'Fragmentation and Consolidation: The Contrasting Cases of Somali and Kurdish Refugees in London', *Journal of Refugee Studies*, 13:3, 281–302.

Gündoğan, Azat Z. (2011) 'Space, State-Making and Contentious Kurdish Politics in Turkey: The Case of Eastern Meetings', *Journal of Balkan and Near Eastern Studies*, 13:4, 389–416.

Gunes, Cengiz (2012) *The Kurdish National Movement in Turkey: From Protest to Resistance*, Abingdon: Routledge.

Gunes, Cengiz (2017) 'Turkey's New Left', *New Left Review*, 107, 9–30.

Gunes, Cengiz (2019) *The Kurds in a New Middle East: The Changing Geopolitics of a Regional Conflict*, Cham: Palgrave Macmillan.

Gupta, Rahila (2016) 'Military Fatigues and Floral Scarves', New Internationalist, 1 May, www.newinternationalist.com/features/2016/05/01/rojava-women-syria (accessed 4 January 2021).

Hall, Stuart (1990) 'Cultural Identity and Diaspora', in Jonathan Rutherford (ed.), *Identity: Community, Culture, Difference*, London: Lawrence and Wishart, pp. 222–37.

Hall, Stuart (1996) 'Introduction: Who Needs 'Identity'?' in Stuart Hall and Paul du Gay (eds), *Questions of Identity*, Thousand Oaks, CA: Sage, pp. 1–17.

Hall, Stuart (2000) 'Conclusion: Multi-cultural Question', in Barnor Hesse (ed.), *Un/Settled Multiculturalism: Diasporas, Entanglements, Transruptions*, London: Zed Books, pp. 209–41.

Hall, Stuart (2006) 'Cosmopolitan Promises, Multicultural Realities', in Richard Scholar (ed.), *Divided Cities: The Oxford Amnesty Lectures 2003*, Oxford: Oxford University Press, pp. 20–51.

Hall, Stuart (2007) 'Living with Difference: Stuart Hall in Conversation with Bill Schwarz', *Soundings*, 37, 148–58.

Hannoum, Abdelmajid (2003) 'Translation and The Colonial Imaginary: Ibn Khaldûn Orientalist', *History and Theory*, 42:1, 61–81.

Hassanpour, Amir and Shahrzad Mojab (2004) 'Kurdish Diaspora', in Melvin Ember, Carol R. Ember and Ian Skoggard (eds), *Encyclopaedia of Diasporas: Immigrant and Refugee Cultures Around the World*, Guildford: Springer, pp. 214–24.

Heath, Anthony and Demireva, Neli (2014) 'Has Multiculturalism Failed in Britain?', *Ethnic and Racial Studies*, 37:1, 161–80.

Henehan, Kathleen and Rose, Helena (2018) *Opportunities Knocked? Exploring Pay Penalties Among the UK's Ethnic Minorities*, London: Resolution Foundation, www.resolutionfoundation.org/app/uploads/2018/07/Opportunities-Knocked.pdf(accessed 4 January 2021).

Henley, Jon (2016) 'White and Wealthy Voters Gave Victory to Donald Trump, Exit Polls Show', *The Guardian*, 9 November, www.theguardian.com/us-news/2016/nov/09/white-voters-victory-donald-trump-exit-polls (accessed 4 January 2021).

Hesse, Barnor (2000) 'Introduction: Un/Settled Multiculturalisms', in Barnor Hesse (ed.), *Un/Settled Multiculturalism: Diasporas, Entanglements, Transruptions*, London: Zed Books, pp. 1–30.

Hirsh, Afua (2018) *Brit(ish): On Race, Identity and Belonging*, London: Vintage.

Hochschild, Arlie Russell (2016) *Strangers in Their Own Land*, New York: The New Press.

Holmwood, John (2020) '"White Nation" Conservatism', *Discover Society*, May, https://archive.discoversociety.org/2020/05/06/viewpoint-white-nation-conservatism(accessed 4 January 2021).

Holmwood, John and O'Toole, Therese (2017) *Countering Extremism in British Schools? The Truth about the Birmingham Trojan Horse Affair*, Bristol: Policy Press.

Holmwood, John and Stewart, Alexander (1991) *Explanation and Social Theory*, Basingstoke: Palgrave.

hooks, bell (1995) '"This is the Oppressor's Language/Yet I Need It to Talk to You": Language, a Place of Struggle', in Anuradha Dingwaney and Carol Maier (eds), *Between Languages and Cultures*, Pittsburgh, PA: University of Pittsburgh Press, pp. 295–301.

Houston, Christopher (2004) 'Creating Diaspora Within a Country: Kurds in Turkey', in Melvin Ember, Carol R. Ember and Ian Skoggard (eds) *Encyclopaedia of Diasporas: Immigrant and Refugee Cultures Around the World*, Guildford: Springer, pp. 403–11.

Human Rights Watch (2010) 2010 Report, www.hrw.org/report/2010/11/01/protesting-terrorist-offense/arbitrary-use-terrorism-laws-prosecute-and (accessed 4 January 2021).

Human Rights Watch (2012) 2012 Report, www.hrw.org/report/2012/09/03/time-justice/ending-impunity-killings-and-disappearances-1990s-turkey (accessed 4 January 2021).

Hussain, Yasmin (2016 [2005]) *Writing Diaspora: South Asian Women, Culture and Ethnicity*, London: Routledge.

Hussain, Shilan Fuad (2020) 'Turkey's Kurdish Minority Art: Its Expression in Modern Times' *Archivi di Studi Indo-Mediterranei*, http://archivindomed.altervista.org/ASIM-10_Shilan.pdf (accessed 31 July 2021).

Hutchinson, Jo, Boneet, Sara, Crenna-Jennings, Whitney and Akhal, Avinash (2019) *Education in England: Annual Report 2019*, London: Education Policy Institute, epi.org.uk/wp-content/uploads/2019/07/EPI-Annual-Report-2019.pdf(accessed 4 January 2021).

Hutnyk, John (2005) 'Hybridity', *Ethnic and Racial Studies*, 28:1, 79–102.

Huxtable, Sally-Anne , Fowler, Corinne , Kefalas, Christo and Slocombe, Emma (2020) *Interim Report on the Connections Between Colonialism and Properties Now in the Care of the National Trust, Including Links with Historic Slavery*, London: National Trust (UK).

Inglehart, Ronald and Norris, Pippa (2016) 'Trump, Brexit, and the Rise of Populism: Economic Have-Nots and Cultural Backlash', www.hks.harvard.edu/publications/trump-brexit-and-rise-populism-economic-have-nots-and-cultural-backlash (accessed 4 January 2021).

Institut National d'Etudes Démographiques – INED (2020) 'Immigrant and Foreign Population', www.ined.fr/en/everything_about_population/data/france/immigrants-foreigners/immigrants-foreigners (accessed 4 January 2021).

International Crisis Group Report (2012) *Turkey: The PKK and a Kurdish Settlement*, www.crisisgroup.org/europe-central-asia/western-europemediterranean/turkey/turkey-pkk-and-kurdish-settlement (accessed 4 January 2021).

Inwood, Joshua (2019) 'White Supremacy, White Counter-Revolutionary Politics, and the Rise of Donald Trump', *Politics and Space*, 37:4, 579–96.

Jacquemond, Richard (1992) 'Translation and Cultural Hegemony: The Case of French-Arabic Translation', in Lawrence Venuti (ed.), *Rethinking Translation: Discourse, Subjectivity, Ideology*, London: Routledge, pp. 139–58.

Jardina, Ashley (2019) *White Identity Politics*, Cambridge: Cambridge University Press.

Jenkins, Celia (2020) '"Aspirational Capital" and Transformations in First-generation Alevi-Kurdish Parents' Involvement with Their Children's Education in the UK', *Kurdish Studies*, 8:1, 163–84.

Jenkins, Celia and Cetin, Umit (2017) 'From a "Sort of Muslim" to "Proud to be Alevi": The Alevi Religion and Identity Project Combatting the Negative Identity Among Second-Generation Alevis in the UK', *National Identities*, 20:1, 105–23.

Jones, Hannah, Gunaratnam, Yasmin, Bhattacharyya, Gargi, Davies, William, Dhaliwal, Sukhwant, Forkert, Kirsten, Jackson, Emma and Saltus, Roiyah (2017) *Go Home? The Politics of Immigration Controversies*, Manchester: Manchester University Press.

Joseph-Salisbury, Remi (2018) *Black Mixed-Race Men: Transatlanticity, Hybridity and 'Post-Racial' Resilience*, Bingley: Emerald.

Jump, Robert Calvert and Michell, Jo (2020) 'Deprivation and the Electoral Geography of Brexit', *SSRN*, https://papers.ssrn.com/sol3/papers.cfm?abstract_id=3727280(accessed 4 January 2021).

Karamcheti, Indira (1995) 'Aime Cesaire's Subjective Geographies: Translating Place and the Difference It Makes', in Anuradha Dingwaney and Carol Maier (eds), *Between Languages and Cultures: Translation and Cross-cultural Texts*, Pittsburgh, PA: University of Pittsburgh Press, pp. 181–97.

Karatani, Rieko (2003) *Defining British Citizenship: Empire, Commonwealth, and Modern Britain*, London: Frank Cass.

Kaufmann, Eric (2017) *'Racial Self-interest' is Not Racism: Ethno-Demographic Interests and the Immigration Debate*, London: Policy Exchange, policyexchange.org.uk/wp-content/uploads/2017/03/Racial-Self-Interest-is-not-Racism-FINAL.pdf(accessed 4 January 2021).

Kaufmann, Eric (2018) *Whiteshift: Populism, Immigration and the Future of White Majorities*, Harmondsworth: Penguin.

Keles, Janroj Y. (2015) *Media, Diaspora, and Conflict: Nationalism and Identity Amongst Turkish and Kurdish Migrants in Europe*, London: I.B. Tauris.

Kenny, Kevin (2013) *Diaspora: A Very Short Introduction*, Oxford: Oxford University Press.

Khan, Omar (2018) '2011 Runnymede Comments on "Gangs" and the UK Riots', Race Matters, www.runnymedetrust.org/blog/2011-runnymede-comments-on-gangs-and-the-uk-riots (accessed 4 January 2021).

Khan, Yasmin (2015) *The Raj at War: A People's History of India's Second World War*, London: Bodley Head.

Khan, Yasmin (2017) 'Dunkirk, the War and the Amnesia of the Empire', New York Times, 2 August www.nytimes.com/2017/08/02/opinion/dunkirk-indians-world-war.html?smid=fb-share&referer=http%253A%252F%252Fm.facebook.com&fbclid=IwAR1GDjUR5WOJsXkRcJylsN6JOuo5AY4o1nhO3SQz4zMMTr1-L4Q9fUlWaUQ (accessed 4 January 2021).

King, Russell, Thomson, Mark, Mai, Nicola and Keles, Yilmaz (2008) *'Turks' in London: Shades of Invisibility and the Shifting Relevance of Policy in the Migration Process*, University of Sussex: Sussex Centre for Migration Research, sro.sussex.ac.uk/id/eprint/11545/1/mwp51.pdf (accessed 4 January 2021).

Kirwan-Taylor, Helen (2000) 'The Cosmocrats', *Harpers and Queen*, October, 188–91.

Kuhn, Thomas S. (1996 [1962]) *The Structure of Scientific Revolutions*, Chicago: Chicago University Press.

Kurdish Institute (2016) 'Kurdish Diaspora', www.institutkurde.org/en/info/kurdish-diaspora-1232550988 (accessed 4 January 2021).

Kurdish Institute (2017) 'The Kurdish Population', www.institutkurde.org/en/info/the-kurdish-population-1232551004 (accessed 4 January 2021).

Kusch, Martin (2002) *Knowledge by Agreement: The Programme of Communitarian Epistemology*, Oxford: Oxford University Press.

Kushnick, Louis (1993) '"We're Here Because You Were There": Britain's Black Population', *Trotter Review*, 7:2, 17–19.

Lammy, David (2019) 'Speeches on the Windrush Scandal in Parliament', www.davidlammy.co.uk/single-post/2018/05/29/Speeches-on-the-Windrush-crisis-in-Parliament (accessed 4 January 2021).

Leach, Edmund R. (1954) *Political Systems of Highland Burma*, London: Bell.

Lefevere, André (1992) *Translation, Rewriting, and the Manipulation of Literary Fame*, London: Routledge.

Leggewie, Claus (1996) 'How Turks Became Kurds, Not Germans', *Dissent*, 43:3, 79–83.

Lentin, Alana and Titley, Gavan (2011) *The Crises of Multiculturalism: Racism in a Neoliberal Age*, London: Zed Books.

Levander, Caroline and Mignolo, Walter (2011) 'Introduction: The Global South and World Dis/Order', *The Global South*, 5:1, 1–11.

Lévy-Bruhl, Lucien (1985) *How Natives Think*, trans. Lilian A. Clare, Princeton, NJ: Princeton University Press.

Lotem, Itay (2016) 'Anti-Racist Activism and the Memory of Colonialism: Race as Republican Critique after 2005', *Modern and Contemporary France*, 24:3, 283–98.

Macaulay, Thomas B. (1995) 'Minute on Indian Education', in Bill Ashcroft, Gareth Griffiths and Helen Tiffin (eds), *The Post-Colonial Studies Reader*, London: Routledge, pp. 428–30.

Mahmod, Jowan (2016) *Kurdish Diaspora Online: From Imagined Community to Managing Communities*, London: Palgrave Macmillan.

Maitland, Sarah (2017) *What is Cultural Translation?*, London: Bloomsbury.

Makoni, Sinfree B. (2012) 'A Critique of Language, Languaging and Supervernacular', *Muitas Vozes*, 1:2, 189–99.

Mandela, Nelson (1997) 'Nelson Mandela's Message for Kurds', www.youtube.com/watch?v=MEI6uaEsKgI&feature=youtu.be   (accessed 4 January 2021).

Martin, Natalie (2018) 'The A.K. Party and the Kurds since 2014: A Discourse of Terror', *British Journal of Middle Eastern Studies*, 45:4, 543–58.

Mavroudi, Elizabeth (2008) 'Palestinians in Diaspora: Empowerment and Informal Political Space', *Political Geography*, 27, 57–73.

Mayblin, Lucy (2017) *Asylum After Empire: Colonial Legacies in the Politics of Asylum Seeking*, London: Rowman and Littlefield.

Mayblin, Lucy and James, Poppy (2019) 'Asylum and Refugee Support in the UK: Civil Society Filling the Gaps?', *Journal of Ethnic and Migration Studies*, 45:3, 375–94.

Meer, Nasar (2015) *Citizenship, Identity & the Politics of Multiculturalism*, Basingstoke: Palgrave Macmillan.

Melville, James (2020) 'The Fake Superiority and Inferiority Complex of Brexit', *Byline Times*, bylinetimes.com/2020/01/31/the-fake-superiority-and-inferiority-complex-of-brexit/?fbclid=IwAR0noZGtPv-OD8Yw5Ajbgxd6_j7sYvfVWu7alD14YlPCsKdTFp4pC2pCrII(accessed 4 January 2021).

Mercer, Kobena (1988) 'Diaspora Culture and the Dialogic Imagination: The Aesthetics of Black Independent Film in Britain', in Mbye B. Cham and Claire Andrade-Watkins (eds), *Blackframes: Critical Perspectives on Black Independent Cinema*, Cambridge, MA: MIT Press, pp. 50–61.

Mercer, Kobena (1994) *Welcome to the Jungle: New Positions in Black Cultural Studies*, New York: Routledge.

Merz, Beverly (1985) 'Nobelists take Genetics from Bench to Bedside'. *The Journal of the American Medical Association*, 254:22, 3161.

Metropolitan Police Service (2012) 4 Days in August: Strategic Review into the Disorders of August 2011 – Final Report, www.slideshare.net/nuzhound/metropolitan-police-service-report-4-days-in-august (accessed 4 January 2021).

Miah, Shamim (2017) *Muslims, Schooling and Security Trojan Horse, Prevent and Racial Politics,* Cham: Palgrave Macmillan.

Miah, Shamim, Sanderson, Pete and Thomas, Paul (2020) 'Race', Space and Multiculturalism in Northern England: The M62 corridor of Uncertainty,* Cham: Palgrave Macmillan.

Micklethwait, John and Wooldridge, Adrian (2003) *A Future Perfect: The Challenge and Promise of Globalization,* New York: Random House.

Mill, John Stuart (1869) *The Subjection of Women.* London: Longmans, Green, Reader and Dyer.

Ministry of Justice (2012), Statistical Bulletin on the Public Disorder of 6th to 9th August 2011, www.gov.uk/government/statistics/statistical-bulletin-on-the-public-disorder-of-6th-9th-august-2011--2 (accessed 4 January 2021).

Mishra, Sudesh (2006) *Diaspora Criticism,* Edinburgh: Edinburgh University Press.

Mitchell, Gemma and Demir, Ipek (2021) 'Translating Risk: How Social Workers' Epistemological Assumptions Shape the Way They Share Knowledge', *Health, Risk & Society,* 23, 1–17.

Modood, Tariq (2007) *Multiculturalism: A Civic Idea,* Cambridge: Polity Press.

Mondon, Aurelien and Winter, Aaron (2019) 'Whiteness, Populism and the Racialisation of the Working Class in the United Kingdom and the United States', *Identities: Global Studies in Culture and Power,* 26:5, 510–28.

Mondon, Aurelien and Winter, Aaron (2020) 'Whiteness, Populism and the Racialisation of the Working Class in the United Kingdom and the United States', *Identities Blog,* www.identitiesjournal.com/blog-articles/whiteness-populism-and-the-racialisation-of-the-working-class-in-the-united-kingdom-and-the-united-states (accessed 4 January 2021).

Monforte, Pierre (2016) 'The Border as a Space of Contention: The Spatial Strategies of Protest Against Border Controls in Europe', *Citizenship Studies,* 20:3–4, 411–26.

Moore, Charles (2020) 'The National Trust's Shameful Manifesto', *Spectator,* 26 September, www.spectator.co.uk/article/the-national-trusts-shameful-manifesto (accessed 4 January 2021).

Mosley, Albert (2017) '"Race" in Eighteenth and Nineteenth Century Discourse by Africans in the Diaspora' in Naomi Zack (ed.), *Oxford Handbook of Philosophy and Race,* New York: Oxford University Press, pp. 81–90.

Murji, Karim (2008) 'Mis-taken Identity: Being and not being Asian, African and British', *Migrations & Identities,* 1:2, 17–32.

Murray, Charles (1990) *The Emerging British Underclass,* London: Institute for Economic Affairs.

Murray, Charles (1996) *Charles Murray and the Underclass: The Developing Debate,* Lancing: Hartington Fine Arts Ltd, civitas.org.uk/content/files/cw33.pdf (accessed 4 January 2021).

Murray, Charles (2019) 'Underclass Revisited', http://www.aei.org/docLib/20040311_book268text.pdf (accessed 4 January 2021).

Murtagh, Madeleine J., Demir, Ipek, Harris, Jennifer R. and Burton, Paul R. (2011) 'Realizing the Promise of Population Biobanks: A New Model for Translation', *Human Genetics*, 130:3, 333–45.

Muttarak, Raya and Heath, Anthony (2010) 'Who Intermarries in Britain? Explaining Ethnic Diversity in Intermarriage Patterns', *British Journal of Sociology*, 61:2, 275–305.

Mutz, Diana (2018) 'Status Threat, Not Economic Hardship, Explains the 2016 Presidential Vote', *Proceedings of the National Academy of Sciences of the United States of America*, 115:19, E4330–E4339, www.pnas.org/content/115/19/E4330 (accessed 4 January 2021).

Naidoo, Roshi and Littler, Jo (2004) 'White Past, Multicultural Present: Heritage and National Stories', in Helen Brocklehurst and Robert Phillips (eds) *History, Identity and the Question of Britain*, Basingstoke: Palgrave Macmillan, pp. 330–41.

Natali, Denise (2005) *The Kurds and the State: Evolving National Identity in Iraq, Turkey, and Iran*, Syracuse, NY: Syracuse University Press.

Nazroo, James and Kapadia, Dharmi (2013) *The Dynamics of Diversity: Evidence from the 2011 Census,* Manchester: University of Manchester and Joseph Rowntree Foundation Centre on Dynamics of Ethnicity, hummedia.manchester.ac.uk/institutes/code/briefingsupdated/Ethnic%20inequalities%20in%20labour%20market%20participation.pdf(accessed 4 January 2021).

New York Times (2020) 'National Exit Polls: How Different Groups Voted?', www.nytimes.com/interactive/2020/11/03/us/elections/exit-polls-president.html?0p19G=0232 (accessed 4 January 2021).

Newburn, Tim, Cooper, Kerris, Deacon, Rachel and Diski, Beka (2015) 'Shopping for Free? Looting, Consumerism and the 2011 Riots', *British Journal of Criminology*, 55, 987–1004.

Nightingale, Carl Husemoller (1993) *On the Edge: A History of Poor Black Children and Their American Dreams,* New York: Basic Books.

Niranjana, Tejaswini (1992) *Siting Translation: History, Post-structuralism, and the Colonial Context*, Berkeley, CA: University of California Press.

Norris, Pippa and Inglehart, Ronald F. (2019) *Cultural Backlash: Trump, Brexit and Authoritarian Populism,* Cambridge: Cambridge University Press.

O'Neill, Veronica (2011) 'The Underlying Role of Translation: A Discussion of Walter Benjamin's "Kinship"', in Lisa Foran (ed.), *Translation and Philosophy*, Bern: Peter Lang, pp. 125–38.

Ong, Aihwa and Nonini, Donald M. (1997) 'Toward a Cultural Politics of Diaspora and Transnationalism', in Aihwa Ong and Donald Nonini (eds), *Ungrounded Empires: The Cultural Politics of modern Chinese Transnationalism,* New York: Routledge, pp. 323–32.

Open Society Institute (2010) *Muslims in Leicester*, London: Open Society Institute, www.opensocietyfoundations.org/sites/default/files/a-muslims-leicester-20110106_0.pdf (accessed 4 January 2021).

Østergaard-Nielsen, Eva K. (2001) 'Transnational Political Practices and the Receiving State: Turks and Kurds in Germany and the Netherlands', *Global Networks*, 1:3, 261–81.

Ostrand, Nicole (2015) 'The Syrian Refugee Crisis: A Comparison of Responses by Germany, Sweden, the United Kingdom, and the United States', *Journal on Migration and Human Security*, 3:3, 255–79.

Özok-Gündoğan, Nilay (2014) 'Ruling the Periphery, Governing the Land: The Making of the Modern Ottoman State in Kurdistan, 1840–1870', *Comparative Studies of South Asia, Africa and the Middle East*, 34:1, 160–75.

Özok-Gündoğan, Nilay (2020) 'Counting the Population and the Wealth in an "Unruly" Land: Census Making as a Social Process in Ottoman Kurdistan, 1830–50', *Journal of Social History*, 53:3, 763–91.

Papineau, David (1978) *For Science in the Social Sciences*, London: Palgrave Macmillan.

Parekh, Bhikhu (2000) *Rethinking Multiculturalism: Cultural Diversity and Political Theory*, London: Palgrave Macmillan.

Pearce, Lynne, Fowler, Corinne and Crawshaw, Robert (2013) *Postcolonial Manchester: Devolved Literary Cultures*, Manchester: Manchester University Press.

Phillips, Trevor (2016) *Race and Faith: The Deafening Silence*, London: Civitas, www.civitas.org.uk/content/files/Race-and-Faith.pdf (accessed 4 January 2021).

Pitts, Johny (2020) *Afropean: Notes from Black Europe*, Harmondsworth: Penguin.

Polezzi, Loredana (2012) 'Translation and Migration', *Translation Studies*, 5:3, 346–57.

Policy Exchange (2017) '"Racial Self-Interest" is Not Racism', policyexchange.org.uk/publication/racial-self-interest-is-not-racism(accessed 4 January 2021).

Polit, Denise F. and Beck, Cheryl T. (2010) 'Generalization in Quantitative and Qualitative Research: Myths and Strategies', *International Journal of Nursing Studies*, 47:11, 1451–8.

Prabhat, Devyani (2019) 'Shamima Begum: Legality of revoking British Citizenship of Islamic State Teenager Hangs on Her Heritage', The Conversation, 21 February, https://theconversation.com/shamima-begum-legality-of-revoking-british-citizenship-of-islamic-state-teenager-hangs-on-her-heritage-112163(accessed 4 January 2021).

Project 2021 (2021) Colonial Countryside Project, www2.le.ac.uk/departments/english/creativewriting/centre/colonial-countryside-project (accessed 4 January 2021).

Rae, Alasdair (2016) 'What Can Explain Brexit?' Stats, Maps n Pix, June, www.statsmapsnpix.com/2016/06/what-can-explain-brexit.html(accessed 4 January 2021).

Rafael, Vicente L. (1993) *Contracting Colonialism: Translation and Christian Conversion in Tagalog Society Under Early Spanish Rule*, Durham, NC: Duke University Press.

Ricoeur, Paul (2006) *On Translation*, trans. Eileen Brennan, London: Routledge.

Ricoeur, Paul (2007) *Reflections of the Just*, trans. David Pellauer, Chicago, IL: University of Chicago Press.

Robinson, Douglas (1997) *Translation and Empire*, London: Routledge.

Roediger, David R. (2007 [1991]) *The Wages of Whiteness: Race and the Making of the American Working Class*, London: Verso.

Roediger, David R. (2017) 'Who's Afraid of the White Working Class? On Joan C. Williams's 'White Working Class: Overcoming Class Cluelessness in America', *Los Angeles Review of Books*, https://lareviewofbooks.org/article/whos-afraid-of-the-white-working-class-on-joan-c-williamss-white-working-class-overcoming-class-cluelessness-in-america (accessed 4 January 2021).

Safran, William (1991) 'Diasporas in Modern Societies: Myths of Homeland and Return', *Diaspora*, 1:1, 83–99.

Said, Edward (1978) *Orientalism*. New York: Pantheon.

Saraçoğlu, Cenk (2010) 'The Changing Image of the Kurds in Turkish Cities: Middle-class Perceptions of Kurdish Migrants in Izmir', *Patterns of Prejudice*, 44:3, 239–60.

Sarıtaş, B. Siynem Ezgi (2010) 'Articulation of Kurdish Identity Through Politicized Music of Koms', Master's thesis, Ankara: METU, etd.lib. metu.edu.tr/upload/12611651/index.pdf(accessed 4 January 2021).

Sayer, Derek (2017) 'White Riot – Brexit, Trump, and Post-Factual Politics', *Journal of Historical Sociology*, 30:1, 92–106.

Sayyid, Salman (2000a) 'Bad Faith: Anti-Essentialism, Universalism and Islamism', in Avtar Brah and Annie E. Coombes (eds), *Hybridity and Its Discontents: Politics, Science, Culture*, London: Routledge, Ch. 12.

Sayyid, Salman (2000b) 'Beyond Westphalia: Nations and Diasporas – the Case of the Muslim *Umma*', in Barnor Hesse (ed.), *Un/Settled Multiculturalism: Diasporas, Entanglements, Transruptions*, London: Zed Books, pp. 33–50.

Shain, Yossi and Barth, Aharon (2003) 'Diasporas and International Relations Theory', *International Organization*, 57:3, 449–79.

Sheffer, Gabriel (1986) 'A New Field of Study: Modern Diasporas in International Politics', in Gabriel Sheffer (ed.), *Modern Diasporas in International Politics*, London: Croom Helm, pp. 1–15.

Sheffer, Gabriel (2003) *Diaspora Politics: At Home Abroad*, Cambridge: Cambridge University Press.

Shilliam, Robbie (2015) *The Black Pacific: Anticolonial Struggles and Oceanic Connections*, London: Bloomsbury.

Shilliam, Robbie (2018) *Race and the Undeserving Poor*, Newcastle upon Tyne: Agenda.

Shilliam, Robbie (2020) 'Redeeming the "Ordinary Working Class"', *Current Sociology*, 68:2, 223–40.

Shukla, Nikesh (2017) *The Good Immigrant*, London: Unbound.

Shuval, Judith T. (2000) 'Diaspora Migration: Definitional Ambiguities and a Theoretical Paradigm', *International Migration* 38:5, 41–56.

Siegel, James T. (1993 [1986]) *Solo in the New Order: Language and Hierarchy in an Indonesian City*, Princeton, NJ: Princeton University Press.

Simon, Sherry (1996) *Gender in Translation: Cultural Identity and the Politics of Transmission*, New York: Routledge.

Şimşek, Dogus (2017) 'Turkey as a "Safe Third Country"? The Impacts of the EU–Turkey Statement on Syrian refugees in Turkey', *Journal of International Affairs: Perception*, 22:4, 161–82.

Singh, Sunny (2017) 'Why the Lack of Indian and African Faces in Dunkirk Matters', The Guardian, 1 August, www.theguardian.com/commentisfree/2017/aug/01/indian-african-dunkirk-history-whitewash-attitudes (accessed 4 January 2021).

Sivanandan, Ambalavaner (1982) *A Different Hunger: Writings on Black Resistance*, London: Pluto Press.

Slater, Tom (2012) 'The Myth of "Broken Britain": Welfare Reform and the Production of Ignorance', *Antipode*, 46:4, 948–69.

Snell-Hornby, Mary (1988) *Translation Studies: An Integrated Approach*, Amsterdam: John Benjamins.

Snoussi, Dhelia and Mompelat, Laurie (2019) '"We are Ghosts": Race, Class and Institutional Prejudice', *Runnymede Class Report*, www.runnymedetrust.org/uploads/publications/We%20Are%20Ghosts.pdf (accessed 4 January 2021).

Sobolewska, Maria and Ford, Robert (2019) 'British Culture Wars? Brexit and the Future Politics of Immigration and Ethnic Diversity', *The Political Quarterly*, 90:2, 142–54.

Soguk, Nevzat (2008) 'Transversal Communication, Diaspora, and the Euro-Kurds', *Review of International Studies*, 34, 173–92.

Solomos, John and Back, Les (1996) *Racism and Society*, Basingstoke: Macmillan.

Soysal, Yasemin Nuhoglu (2000) 'Citizenship and Identity: Living in Diasporas in Post-War Europe', *Ethnic and Racial Studies*, 23:1, 1–15.

Spivak, Gayatri (2004 [1993]) 'The Politics of Translation', in Lawrence Venuti (ed.), *Translation Studies Reader*, London: Routledge, pp. 369–88.

Storm, Ingrid, Sobolewska, Maria and Ford, Robert (2017) 'Is Ethnic Prejudice declining in Britain? Change in Social Distance Attitudes among Ethnic Majority and Minority Britons', *The British Journal of Sociology*, 68:3, 410–34.

Tate, Shirley Anne (2005) *Black Skins, Black Masks: Hybridity, Dialogism, Performativity*, Aldershot: Ashgate.

Taylor, Charles (1992) 'The Politics of Recognition', in Amy Gutmann (ed.), *Multiculturalism and the Politics of Recognition*, Princeton, NJ: Princeton University Press.

Thangaraj, Stanley (2019) 'Kurdish Diasporic Matters: Signalling New Epistemologies of Difference', *Journal of Ethnic and Cultural Studies*, 6:2, 1–10.

Thobani, Sitara (2019) 'Alt-Right with the Hindu-right: Long-Distance Nationalism and the Perfection of Hindutva', *Ethnic and Racial Studies* 42:5, 745–62.

Tilley, Lisa (2017) 'The Making of the "White Working Class": Where Fascist Resurgence Meets Leftist White Anxiety', *Wildcat Dispatches* (blog), http://wildcatdispatches.org/?p=24 (accessed 4 September 2020).

Timmermans, Stefan and Tavory, Iddo (2012) 'Theory Construction in Qualitative Research: From Grounded Theory to Abductive Analysis', *Sociological Theory*, 30:3, 167–86.

Titley, Gavan (2020) *Is Free Speech Racist?*, Cambridge: Polity Press.

Toivanen, Mari and Başer, Bahar (2019) 'Remembering the Past in Diasporic Spaces: Kurdish Reflection on Genocide Memoralization for Anfal', *Genocide Studies International*, 13:1, 10–33.

Tölölyan, Khachig (1996) 'Rethinking Diaspora(s): Stateless Power in the Transnational Moment', *Diaspora*, 5:1, 3–35.

Tölölyan, Khachig (2019) 'Diaspora Studies: Past, Present and Promise', in Robin Cohen and Carolin Fischer (eds), *Routledge Handbook of Diaspora Studies*, London: Routledge, pp. 22–30.

Trivedi, Harish (2005) 'Translating Culture vs Cultural Translation', *91st Meridian*, 4:1, https://iwp.uiowa.edu/91st/vol4-num1/translating-culture-vs-cultural-translation(accessed 4 January 2021).

Trouillot, Michel-Rolph (1995) *Silencing the Past: Power and Production of History*, Boston, MA: Beacon Press.

Tsuda, Takeyuki (2019) 'Diasporicity: Relative Embeddedness in Transnational and co-Ethnic Networks', in Robin Cohen and Carolin Fischer (eds), *Routledge Handbook of Diaspora Studies*, London: Routledge, pp. 189–96.

Tymoczko, Maria (1999) 'Post-colonial Writing and Literary Translation', in Susan Bassnett and Harish Trivedi (eds), *Post-Colonial Translation: Theory and Practice*, London: Routledge, pp. 19–40.

Tymoczko, Maria (2007) *Enlarging Translating, Empowering Translators*, Manchester: Jerome Publishing.

Tymoczko, Maria and Gentzler, Edwin (eds) (2002) *Translation and Power*, Amherst, MA: University of Massachusetts Press.

UKIP (2017) *Britain Together: UK 2017 Manifesto*. www.ukip.org/manifesto2017(accessed 25 July 2021).

United Nations High Commission for Human Rights (2017) Report on the Human Rights Situation in South-East Turkey www.ohchr.org/Documents/Countries/TR/OHCHR_South-East_TurkeyReport_10March2017.pdf (accessed 4 January 2021).

Unlu, Baris (2016) 'The Kurdish Struggle and the Crisis of the Turkishness Contract', *Philosophy and Social Criticism*, 42:4–5, 397–405.

Vali, Abbas (2014) *Kurds and the State in Iran: The Making of Kurdish Identity*, London: Bloomsbury.

Venuti, Lawrence (ed.) (1992) *Rethinking Translation: Discourse, Subjectivity, Ideology*, London: Routledge.

Venuti, Lawrence (1995) *The Translator's Invisibility: A History of Translation*, London: Routledge.

Venuti, Lawrence (2002) *The Scandals of Translation*, London: Routledge.

Vertovec, Steven (2007) 'Super-diversity and Its Implications', *Ethnic and Racial Studies*, 30:6, 1024–54.

Viera, Else Ribeiro Pires (1999) 'Liberating Calibans: Readings of Antropofagia and Harolde de Campos' Poetics of Transcreation' in Susan Bassnett and Harish Trivedi (eds), *Post-Colonial Translation: Theory and Practice*, London: Routledge, pp. 95–113.

Virdee, Satnam (2014) *Racism, Class and the Racialized Outsider*, Basingstoke: Palgrave Macmillan.

Virdee, Satnam and McGeever, Brendan (2018) 'Racism, Crisis, Brexit', *Ethnic and Racial Studies*, 41:10, 1802–19.

Visram, Rozina (1986) *Ayahs, Lascars and Princes: Indians in Britain, 1700–1947*, London: Pluto Press.

Von Flotow, Luise (1991) 'Feminist Translation: Contexts, Practices and Theories', *Traduction, Terminologie et Redaction*, 4:2, 69–84.

Wahlbeck, Östen (1998) 'Community Work and Exile Politics: Kurdish Refugee Associations in London', *Journal of Refugee Studies*, 11:3, 215–30.

Wahlbeck, Östen (2002) 'The Concept of Diaspora as an Analytical Tool in the Study of Refugee Communities', *Journal of Ethnic and Migration Studies*, 28:2, 221–38.

Watts, Nicole F. (2010) 'The Missing Moderate: Legitimacy Resources and Pro-Kurdish Party Politics in Turkey', in Robert Lowe and Gareth Stansfield (eds), *The Kurdish Policy Imperative*, London: Chatham House, pp. 97–115.

Wemyss, Georgie (2009) *The Invisible Empire: White Discourse, Tolerance and Belonging*, London: Routledge.

Werbner, Pnina (1997) 'Introduction: The Dialectics of Cultural Hybridity', in Pnina Werbner and Tariq Modood (eds), *Debating Cultural Hybridity: Multi-Cultural Identities and the Politics of Anti-Racism*, London: Zed Press, pp. 1–27.

Wessendorf, Suzanne (2016) 'Settling in a Super-Diverse Context: Recent Migrants' Experiences of Conviviality', *Journal of Intercultural Studies*, 37:5, 449–63.

White, James Boyd (1995) 'On the Virtues of Not Understanding', in Anuradha Dingwaney and Carol Maier (eds), *Between Languages and Cultures*, Pittsburgh, PA: University of Pittsburgh Press, pp. 333–9.

White, Paul J. (2007) 'Citizenship Under Ottomans and Kemalists: How the Kurds Were Excluded', *Citizenship Studies*, 3:1, 71–102.

Williams, Jenny (2013) *Theories of Translation*, Basingstoke: Palgrave Macmillan.

Wilson, Bryan (1970) *Rationality*, Oxford: Blackwell.

Winch, Peter (1964) 'Understanding a Primitive Society', *American Philosophical Quarterly*, 1:4, 307–24.

Yeğenoğlu, Meyda (2005) 'Cosmopolitanism and Nationalism in a Globalized World', *Ethnic and Racial Studies*, 28:1, 103–31.

Young, Jock (2003) 'To These Wet and Windy Shores', *Punishment and Society*, 5:4, 449–62.

Yuval-Davis, Nira (2011) *Politics of Belonging: Intersectional Contestations*, London: Sage.

Zephaniah, Benjamin (2009) 'My Family Values', The Guardian, 4 July, www.guardian.co.uk/lifeandstyle/2009/jul/04/benjamin-zephaniah-family-values(accessed 4 January 2021).

Zerhouni, Elias A. (2005) 'Interview: Translational and Clinical Science – Time for a New Vision', *The New England Journal of Medicine*, 353, 1621–3.

Zeydanlıoğlu, Welat (2008) 'The White Turkish Man's Burden: Orientalism, Kemalism and the Kurds in Turkey', in Guido Rings and Anne Ife (eds), *Neo-colonial Mentalities in Contemporary Europe? Language and Discourse in the Construction of Identities*, Newcastle upon Tyne: Cambridge Scholars, pp. 155–74.

Zeydanlıoğlu, Welat (2009) 'Torture and Turkification in the Diyarbakır Military Prison', in John T. Parry and Welat Zeydanlıoğlu (eds), *Rights, Citizenship and Torture: Perspectives on Evil, Law and the State*, Oxford: Inter-Disciplinary Press, pp. 73–92.

Index

EU authorised representative for GPSR:
Easy Access System Europe, Mustamäe tee 50,
10621 Tallinn, Estonia
gpsr.requests@easproject.com

www.ingramcontent.com/pod-product-compliance
Lightning Source LLC
Chambersburg PA
CBHW071028280326
41935CB00011B/1487